D0398356

OLD TESTAMENT
WOMEN

The Storyteller's Companion to the Bible

Michael E. Williams, editor

VOLUME FOUR

OLD TESTAMENT WOMEN

Abingdon Press
Nashville

OLD TESTAMENT WOMEN

Copyright © 1993 by Abingdon Press

All rights reserved.
No part of this work may be reproduced or transmitted in any form or by any means, elec-
tronic or mechanical, including photocopying and recording, or by any information storage
or retrieval system, except as may be expressly permitted by the 1976 Copyright Act or in
writing from the publisher. Requests for permission should be addressed in writing to
Abingdon Press, 201 Eighth Avenue South, Nashville, TN 37203.

This book is printed on recycled, acid-free paper.

Library of Congress Cataloging-in-Publication Data

(Revised for vol. 4)
The Storyteller's companion to the Bible.
    Includes indexes.
    Contents: v. 1. Genesis — v. 2. Exodus-Joshua — [etc.] — v. 4. Old Testament Women.
    1. Bible—Paraphrases, English. 2. Bible—Criticism, interpretation, etc.   I. Williams,
Michael E. (Michael Edward), 1950–
BS550.2.S764   1991   220.9'505   90-26289
ISBN 0-687-39674-3 (v. 4 : alk. paper)

Scripture quotations in "The Story" section of each chapter are from *The Revised English
Bible*. Copyright © 1989 by The Delegates of the Oxford University Press and The Syndics
of the Cambridge University Press. Used by permission.

96 97 98 99 00 01 02 — 10 9 8 7 6 5 4

MANUFACTURED IN THE UNITED STATES OF AMERICA

As always
for
Margaret
and
Sarah
and
now for
Elizabeth

Contributors

Sharon Pace Jeansonne wrote the comments and is Associate Professor of Hebrew Bible in the Department of Theology at Marquette University in Milwaukee, Wisconsin. She is a frequent speaker in synagogues and churches, and her previous publications include *The Women of Genesis: From Sarah to Potiphar's Wife.*

Martha Whitmore Hickman is a children's book author from Nashville, Tennessee. Her previous books include *Fullness of Time: Short Stories of Women and Aging* and *And God Created Squash: How the World Began.*

Betty Lehrman is a professional storyteller from Framingham, Massachusetts, who has "Tales for the Telling." Her storytelling tapes include *Watermelon and Other Stories* and *Jewish Tales from the Heart.*

Michael E. Williams is one of the pastors at Belle Meade United Methodist Church in Nashville, Tennessee. He earned his Ph.D. from Northwestern University and previously directed the preaching office for The United Methodist Church.

Contents

A Storyteller's Companion

Michael E. Williams

This volume, like the previous three in the Storyteller's Companion to the Bible Series, is for anyone interested in telling Bible stories. In this volume we focus our attention on stories of women. Pastors who have preaching responsibilities will find the book particularly helpful as they prepare to tell one of these stories as a part of a sermon. If preaching is to help the listener to participate in the world of the biblical narrative, then telling stories from the Bible is imperative.

In addition, leaders of Bible studies and teachers of church school classes will invariably be called upon to tell Bible stories as part of their lessons. The first three volumes have been used for personal Bible study by many individuals looking for alternative resources for enriching their knowledge of Scripture. It may be that parents or grandparents will want to tell portions of these or other biblical stories at other times, too.

The stories of women in the Bible have not traditionally received the attention they deserve. It is clear from the Hebrew narratives that God employed women as voices to speak God's word and persons to enact God's will. It is also evident that many stories have women acting in both leadership and supporting roles whose presence makes an important difference in the way the story is told as well as its outcome. In this volume, we have chosen to examine stories of women from across the Hebrew Bible and Apocrypha so that their stories might be more effectively told and more clearly heard.

This volume of The Storyteller's Companion is certainly not the first attempt to explore the stories of biblical women. Phyllis Trible's ground-breaking work *Texts of Terror* (Philadelphia: Fortress Press, 1984) includes a thorough examination of four of the stories of women from the Hebrew Bible. Six of the very fine retellings of stories of biblical women in Renita Weems's *Just a Sister Away* (LuraMedia, 1988) are from the Hebrew Bible. Alice Bach and J. Cheryl Exum include Judith from the Apocrypha in their collection of retellings of women's stories from the Hebrew Bible, *Miriam's Well* (Delacorte, 1991).

The present volume does, however, present an extraordinarily comprehensive look at women's stories in the Hebrew Bible with an eye for retelling those stories. We include twenty-seven stories, encompassing the Torah, the Prophets, the Writings, and the Apocrypha (with Judith and Susanna).

9

While we often first encounter these women defined by the relationship to the men in their lives (wives, daughters, mothers, etc.), we soon come to see that they are independent figures, each in her own right. As their portraits become etched in our memories, we can celebrate their joys and grieve their losses. Even for some who never speak a word through their story ("The Silent Concubine"), their very silence clamors for justice. In theater there are three ways we come to know about a character: (1) by what he or she says, (2) by what others say about her or him, or (3) by what the character does. The most trustworthy way to know a character is by far the last of the three.

Nor are these just ancient tales, their significance locked away in some long-lost historical period. These women live today. In his lectures, Joseph Campbell used to assert that the latest embodiment of characters from ancient stories can be seen on any street corner. The prostitutes here still live and work on many city streets; the violence that is inflicted upon the daughter of Jephthah and the concubine is reenacted daily in homes in our communities; and the courageous and virtuous women grace our families even now. Believe me, I know, three such women of courage and virtue grace the household in which I live.

The Stories

While we attempt in this volume to be comprehensive in our approach to women's stories from the Hebrew Bible and the Apocrypha, we obviously could not include them all. While most of the lectionaries of various churches have done a poor job of including stories of women, we have included the texts that appear in *The Revised Common Lectionary*, 1992 (the most inclusive so far). We have gone far beyond the scope of these lectionaries to include stories that make a significant contribution to the biblical narrative as a whole.

If you do not find one of your favorite stories in this collection, there is no need to despair. Much of the information you will learn from the comments on the stories that are included can be transferred to other texts. This will allow you to use your creativity more fully.

The translation from which the printed texts in this companion are taken is *The Revised English Bible*. You may wish to compare the readings here with your favorite translation or several others. It enriches the telling of biblical stories, especially for those who do not read the original language, to work from various translations.

Comments on the Stories

Sharon Pace Jeansonne holds a Ph.D. in Hebrew Bible from the University of Notre Dame and teaches at Marquette University. Her comments reach into the heart of each character and her story, providing both information and perspective for anyone seeking to retell the story. As important as her scholarly insights into these narratives is the profound respect she brings to the biblical narratives and the characters who populate them. Her approach reaches across barriers to women and men who want to honor these women and help them live anew in their preaching and teaching. Jeansonne guides the storyteller through layers of past interpretation, misinterpretation, and neglect of these narratives to provide a fresh starting place for retelling them.

The specific contribution you will make to the preparation for telling one of these stories is knowing your audience. You can take the information Sharon Jeansonne offers and shape a telling of the story that will be appropriate to the ages and life experiences of your listeners. Only you can know where in the lives of those in your congregation, class, or family a story will strike a chord, turn on a light, or heal a hurt. For more information on how to prepare a story for a specific group of listeners, refer to "Learning to Tell Bible Stories: A Self-directed Workshop" on pp. 19-20.

Retelling the Stories

As a storyteller, you will contribute something of your own personality and understanding of the Bible and those of your listeners to the telling of a Bible story. There is no one right way to accomplish this. While this companion includes a sample retelling of each story, these are only examples of one way a story may be told. You may choose to tell it very differently.

The retellings are intended to free your imagination for telling and not to limit you to any one form. Some retellings here are fairly straightforward recountings of a text. Others choose a character or characters from whose point of view to tell the story. Some retellings place the story in the modern world. We hope they will offer you a sample of the vast number of ways Bible stories can come to life in storytelling.

The goal of each retelling is to help our listeners to hear the story as if for the first time and to see the world of the story as something new and fresh. We are grateful for the imaginations of the storytellers who provided the retellings for this volume: Martha Whitmore Hickman is the author of numerous books for adults and children, including *Fullness of Time: Short Stories of Women and Aging* (Nashville: The Upper Room, 1990), which contains her award-winning story, "The Last Hour." She lives in Nashville, Tennessee. Hickman retells the stories of Sarah, Hagar, Rebekah, Rachel, Miriam, Hannah, Bathsheba, and the Sidon widow. Betty Lehrman is a storyteller from Massachusetts who studied theater at Northwestern University and whose tapes of stories have won the Parent's Choice Award. Betty retells the stories of Jephthah's daughter, the wise woman, the prostitutes, the virtuous woman, Esther, Susanna, and Judith. Finally, I retell the stories of Shiphrah and Puah, Dinah, Tamar, Miriam's leprosy, Rahab, Deborah, Samson's mother, the silent concubine, Tamar, Gomer, and Ruth.

Midrashim

If you ask a rabbi a question, you are likely to get a story for an answer. This reflects a wisdom that knows truth to be irreducible to a one-two-three answer. Truth is embodied in events as they happen and in persons as they relate to each other and to God. This kind of truth is best experienced in stories and concrete images. Perhaps no book is a better example of this storied truth telling than the Bible.

The unique contribution this companion makes to the art of biblical story-telling is to include the stories and sayings of the ancient rabbis which relate to the stories of women. These are midrashim (the singular is midrash), from a Hebrew word that means "to go in search of." When the rabbis went in search of the relevance of these already "old, old stories" for their time, they returned with questions. Those questions generated stories that stand alongside the Scripture passages and interpret them in ways that children and adults alike can understand.

The midrashim included here came from several sources, and I have retold and adapted them for inclusion here. These midrashim appear in boxed text in the retelling of each story, placed near the part of the story to which they most closely relate. As you retell the story, you may wish to include one or more of the midrashim at these points in the story or at other appropriate places. For more information, refer to "What Are Midrashim, and What Are They Doing Here?" on pages 00-00.

You will probably not want to read this companion from front to back as you would most books. It is not designed to be read that way. One way to make effective use of it would be first to read Sharon Pace Jeansonne's introduction to her comments on the stories and the introduction to midrash. Then choose a story that you wish to tell. This may be a story from an upcoming Sunday of the lectionary or the church school curriculum, or it may simply be a story that captures your interest. Once you have chosen the story, work through the short workshop on storytelling, using the story you chose as your content.

Use the retelling provided with the story as a guide, but do not feel obligated to simply repeat it. Tell the story for your hearers in your own way. You may choose to include the midrashim with your retelling, or you may tell them afterward. In any case, you are about to take part in one of the most ancient experiences people do in community: offering the gift of God's story so that it touches our story today.

Reading the Narratives About Biblical Women

Sharon Pace Jeansonne

The previous two decades of biblical research have increasingly focused on the importance of women throughout the Bible and in antiquity. This heightened awareness no doubt reflects the interest of society at large with issues of women's equality. Many studies focus on the restrictions and hardships placed on women because of the patriarchal structures of traditional societies as well as on the contributions of women. In the studies of the Hebrew Scriptures, both narrative and poetic texts have been examined to uncover the portrayal of women in all aspects of religious, social, and political life, as well as to reclaim the feminine associations of the God of Israel who is neither male nor female.

The gathering of these lectionary and extra-lectionary texts that feature women is representative of the broad picture of women in the Hebrew Bible and in the Apocrypha. Some of these women's stories were told because of their associations as wives or as mothers of famous men, but nonetheless their accounts witness to their own varied experiences as recipients of God's word, as pursuers of justice, as key players in the drama of Israel's historical memory, or as victims of individual cruelty or the structural evil in the society. The style and content of their stories also give us clues to the narrators' presuppositions and particular concerns. Stereotyping and role restrictions are common: some women are unnamed because they are seen to have lesser prominence than the men with whom they are associated, women are valued for their beauty and their ability to have sons, unmarried women and widows are dependent on men, women hear of God's word through men, women are chastised for challenging male authority, and women are debased as untrustworthy prostitutes or for being sexually promiscuous. Yet women also break through the restrictions and expectations of society to accomplish extraordinary things. Women make possible the fulfillment of God's covenant, risk their lives to save their people, facilitate justice in the community, serve as models of faith, and proclaim words of praise to God.

Because this volume deals with selected stories, it is appropriate to locate each of them in the larger cycles of narrative, poetic sections, or books of the

Bible in which they are found. Thus I often refer to previous or forthcoming appropriate scenes to facilitate familiarity with the broader context, incorporating this material into the commentaries on the texts. This procedure is appropriate for the narrative-critical approach taken in my comments to the stories. I am most interested in uncovering the literary features that comprise the text and serve its artistry and purpose. Setting, word choice, repetition, characterization, dialogue, ambiguity, and point of view are some of the notable features of each account that merit investigation and provide insight into the import of the narrative and the significance of its women both for the ancient audience and for readers today.

Readers will approach these texts with a variety of interests that come from varied experiences and concerns. Some will look for examples of prejudice and stereotyping that hurt women in the past and that may reflect current societal views that cause similar injustices. Others will seek more positive accounts that include women because of their strength of character, dedication to their people, and faith in God, which may be used as evidence that women today have a right to and can expect inclusion in their own religious and social institutions. Both types of searches will be successful. Some accounts uplift one's soul; others enrage it. The stories of women in the Hebrew Bible are valuable not only individually but also because collectively they reflect the variety of women's experience.

What Are Midrashim, and
What Are They Doing Here?

Michael E. Williams

Midrash (the plural in Hebrew is *midrashim*) comes from a Hebrew word meaning "to go in search of" or "to inquire." So midrashim resulted when the ancient rabbis went in search of (inquired into) the meaning of the Scriptures for their lives. Midrash is also the name for the process of inquiring into the Scriptures for their meaning.

We might say that midrash is both our encounter with the biblical stories as we seek their meaning for our lives and times and the stories that emerge to express that meaning. Often midrashim do take the form of stories or pieces of stories (at least the ones we will focus on here do). These stories seek to answer questions about and to fill gaps in the biblical stories.

The midrashim drawn from for this volume come from the period 400–1200 C.E. (what is sometimes called A.D.). They were told, in part, to make the stories of women relevant to a Jewish community that had no homeland, could not hold citizenship in other countries, and experienced hostility and persecution from the outside, including from Christian authorities. Most of these midrashim originated in sermons preached in synagogues, based on the prescribed weekly readings from the Torah (the first five books of the Bible). Others emerged from the popular folk traditions of the Jewish communities. Though they were collected and written during that six-hundred period, there is no way of knowing how long the midrashim had been circulating by word of mouth before someone wrote them down. Some are attributed to rabbis living at the time of Jesus. In fact, certain scholars find evidence that this way of interpreting the Bible has its roots intertwined with the texts of the biblical stories themselves.

I see three basic functions for the midrashim I have selected to be included in this book. The first might be called "filling the gaps." These stories and story fragments answer questions about the biblical stories that the Scripture leaves unanswered. When the rabbis answered such questions, they revealed both their fertile imaginations and their own understanding of God and human beings. Sunday school teachers and college professors will also have encountered these imaginative questions.

The second function of midrash is to draw an analogy. These stories begin with "This may be compared to. . . . " Then the rabbi would tell a contemporary story that exhibited a situation and characters like the biblical story under consideration. You may notice that these stories sometimes bear a resemblance to the parables of Jesus and the *mashal* (parable) form of Jewish teaching.

The third function is to describe an encounter. In these stories someone comes to a rabbi with a question, and the rabbi's response interprets both the biblical story and the situation from which the question emerged. For example, when someone asked a rabbi how Ruth, a Moabite woman, could have been the great-grandmother of King David, since Deuteronomy prohibits a Moabite from every becoming a member of the community, the rabbi responded that the law said Moabite, not Moabitess.

Why did I choose a predominantly Jewish form of interpretation in this book? First, Christians have too often ignored this ancient and time-honored way to interpret the Bible. Given our Jewish roots and Jesus' heritage, midrash is at least as directly related to our tradition as the Greco-Roman philosophy on which we have depended so heavily for ordering our questions and structuring our theological doctrines.

Second, midrashim provide us with a way of interpreting the Bible that involves the imagination and speaks to our experience. It is also, according to certain scholars, the way the Bible interprets itself.

Third, midrashim provide a model for a community-based, inclusive (even children can imaginatively participate in stories), nonprofessional (you don't have to be a trained theologian) way of interpreting the Bible for our times. In short, we can learn the stories the rabbis told about the scriptures to interpret them for their time. In addition, we can follow the example of the rabbis and learn to tell stories about Bible stories that interpret them for our time.

In addition to these reasons I have a personal appreciation for the Jewish storytelling tradition. My intellectual and artistic interests in Jewish narrative range from the Torah to midrash to hasidic stories to modern writers like Isaac Bashevis Singer and Elie Wiesel.

This is just the first step to reclaiming midrashim for modern tellers of Bible stories, but it is a step. If you want to learn more about midrashim related to the stories of Exodus–Joshua, you may wish to read the volumes from which those included here were chosen.

Midrash Rabbah, translated by H. Freedman (London: Soncino Press, 1939), is a ten-volume translation of midrashim on a variety of books of the Bible. There references here, which have been paraphrased and adapted, are to chapter and section. The third edition of this work was published in 1983.

Volume one in Louis Ginzberg's classic collection of stories related to biblical texts, *The Legends of the Jews,* translated by Henrietta Szold (Philadelphia: The Jewish Publication Society, 1909 and 1937), still in print, draws from a wide number of sources, including Christian and Islamic traditions. Here this work, again paraphrased and adapted, is listed as Ginzberg, followed by the volume and page number.

A wonderful addition to the library of persons interested in midrashim is Rabbi William G. Braude's translation of Hayim Naham Bialik and Yehoshua Hana Ravnitzky's *The Book of Legends (Sefer Ha-Aggadah): Legends from the Talmud and Midrash.* References to this work are cited as *Sefer Ha-Aggadah,* followed by the page number and section number.

Another source I have employed is *The Antiquities of the Jews,* by Flavius Josephus. Here again I have paraphrased and adapted these passages and refer to them by book, chapter, and section. In addition, I have found several midrashim in *Mimekor Yishael: Classic Jewish Folktales,* collected by Joseph Bin Gorlon, edited by Emanuel Bin Gorlon, and translated by I. M. Lask (Indiana University Press, 1976).

The most difficult part of assembling this specific collection of stories was finding midrashim to accompany them. In part, this was because we had considered some of the stories in previous volumes, and I did not want to repeat midrashim, if I could help it. I did, however, repeat one in this volume that appears elsewhere in the series. Careful readers, see if you can find it.

The most difficulty came in the limited number of stories the rabbis seem to have told about certain women. There were plenty, for instance, about Ruth and Esther, but I really had to search for midrashim to include alongside the silent concubine. My guess is that the rabbis simply did not want to deal with some of the stories because they were so horrific. Perhaps the sages told fewer stories about women characters, especially those who were not in lead roles, than they did about males. I must admit that this difficulty may, at least in part, be the result of my own limited knowledge of sources for midrashim.

One more word on midrash: For any given passage of Scripture, several stories or interpretations of various rabbis are presented side by side in collections of midrashim. Those who collected these stories saw no reason to decide which was the one right interpretation. This is also true, we might mention, of those who assembled the canon of the New Testament, who saw no reason to choose among the four very different stories about Rabbi Jesus. The understanding behind these choices is that there need be no single correct interpretation. The Bible is viewed as being so inclusive that it could apply to a range of possible life situations. Therefore, we would expect a variety of interpretations to speak to a variety of life situations. Not only the Bible, but also all of its many possible interpretations, are encompassed by the expansive imagination of God. In fact, Solomon, the wisest of all humans, is reputed by the rabbis to have known three thousand stories for every verse of Scripture and one thousand and five interpretations for every story.

Learning to Tell Bible Stories

A Self-directed Workshop

1. Read the story aloud at least twice. You may choose to read the translation included here or the one you are accustomed to reading. I recommend that you examine at least two translations as you prepare, so you can hear the differences in the way they sound when read aloud.

Do read them *aloud*. Yes, if you are not by yourself, people may give you funny looks, but this really is important. Your ear will hear things about the passage that your eye will miss. Besides, you can't skim when you read aloud. You are forced to take your time, and you might notice aspects of the story that you never saw (or heard) before.

As you read, pay special attention to *where* the story takes place, *when* the story takes place, *who* the characters are, *what* objects are important to the story, and the general *order of events* in the story.

2. Now close your eyes and imagine the story taking place. This is your chance to become a playwright/director or screenwriter/filmmaker because you will experience the story on the stage or screen in your imagination. Enjoy this part of the process. It takes only a few minutes, and the budget is within everybody's reach.

3. Look back at the story briefly to make sure you haven't left out any important people, places, things, or events.

4. Try telling the story. This works better if you have someone to listen (even the family pet will do). You can try speaking aloud to yourself or to an imaginary listener. Afterwards ask your listener or yourself what questions arise as a result of this telling. Is the information you need about the people, places, things, or language in the story? Is it appropriate to the age, experiences, and interests of those who will be hearing it? Does the story capture your imagination? One more thing: You don't have to be able to explain the meaning of a story to tell it. In fact, those of the most enduring interest have an element of mystery about them.

5. Read the "Comments on the Story" that Sharon Pace Jeansonne has provided for each passage. Are some of your questions answered there? You may wish also to look at a good Bible dictionary for place names, characters, professions, objects, or words that you need to learn more about. *The Interpreter's*

Dictionary of the Bible (Nashville: Abingdon Press, 1962) is still the most complete source for storytellers.

6. Read the "Retelling the Story" section for the passage you are learning to tell. Does it give you any ideas about how you will tell the story? How would you tell it differently? Would you tell it from another character's point of view? How would that make it a different story? Would you transfer it to a modern setting? What places and characters will you choose to correspond to those in the biblical story? Remember, the retellings that are provided are not meant to be told exactly as they are written here. They are to serve as springboards for your imagination as you develop your telling.

7. Read the midrashim that accompany each retelling. Would you include any of these in your telling? You could introduce them by saying, "This is not in the original story, but the rabbis say. . . . " Do these midrashim respond to any of your questions or relate to any of your life situations or those of your listeners? If so, you might consider using them after the retelling to encourage persons to tell their own stories, which hearing the Bible story has brought to mind. You may even wish to begin creating some modern midrashim of your own or with your listeners.

8. Once you have gotten the elements of the story in mind and have chosen the approach you are going to take in retelling it, you need to practice, practice, practice. Tell the story aloud ten or twenty or fifty times over a period of several days or weeks. Listen as you tell your story. Revise your telling as you go along. Remember that you are not memorizing a text; you are preparing a living event. Each time you tell the story, it will be a little different, because you will be different (if for no other reason than that you have told the story before).

9. The "taste and see" that even the stories of God are good—not all sweet, but good and good for us and for those who hunger to hear.

Sarah

When Sarah at age ninety overhears that she will bear a child, she does the only reasonable thing: She laughs, but later gives birth to Isaac.

The Story

The LORD appeared to Abraham by the terebinths of Mamre, as he was sitting at the opening of his tent in the heat of the day. He looked up and saw three men standing over against him. On seeing them, he hurried from his tent door to meet them. Bowing low he said, 'Sirs, if I have deserved your favour, do not go past your servant without a visit. Let me send for some water so that you may bathe your feet; and rest under this tree, while I fetch a little food so that you may refresh yourselves. Afterwards you may continue the journey which has brought you my way.' They said, 'Very well, do as you say.'

The LORD showed favour to Sarah as he had promised, and made good what he had said about her. She conceived and at the time foretold by God she bore a son to Abraham in his old age. The son whom Sarah bore to him Abraham named Isaac, and when Isaac was eight days old Abraham circumcised him, as decreed by God. Abraham was a hundred years old when his son Isaac was born. Sarah said, 'God has given me good reason to laugh, and everyone who hears will laugh with me.' She added, 'Whoever would have told Abraham that Sarah would suckle children? Yet I have borne him a son in his old age.'

Comments on the Story

Genesis 18 recounts the covenantal promise offered by God to Abraham and Sarah. Abraham, the father of the Jewish people, is the one to whom God first offered the promises of land, descendants, and blessing. But who is this woman who bears his child, and what do we learn of her plight? Is it fair to consider her part of God's covenantal promise, given that God addresses Abraham alone?

Before she features in Genesis 18, Sarah has been introduced earlier as Abraham's barren wife, which is information crucial to the development of the plot. When God promises a son to Abraham, will he be the child of any woman? Sarah's infertility and advanced age allow the reader to doubt her significance in the role of Abraham's offspring. In fact, she cannot believe that

21

God's promises have anything to do with her and devises the plan wherein Abraham is to impregnate her maidservant Hagar, a development that causes Sarah more anguish than she could have imagined. In spite of the situation that makes Sarah a poor candidate to be the mother of Abraham's offspring, the chapter that immediately precedes this selection emphasizes that God's plan differs from Sarah's and Abraham's alternatives. As a symbol of God's covenant, God gives the man named Abram the name Abraham, meaning father of many. Similarly, in popular etymology, Sarah, formerly Sarai, is named by God to signify that she is the princess of a people. In addition, the sign of the covenant is introduced: circumcision. Every man's reproductive organ is to be marked with the sign of God's relationship with Israel. All of this is crucial to understanding the plight of Sarah; yet, in all the revelatory scenes of God's promise to Abraham, there is no indication that God ever revealed the plan to Sarah. Neither is there any account of Abraham's telling of the plan to her. When Abraham hears God's specification that Sarah indeed will bear a son, he falls on his face in laughter!

With this important context identified, we can better clarify the specifics of Genesis 18. In the Hebrew Bible the appearance of God to persons in the form of a divine messenger *(malak)* or messengers occurs frequently. The Hebrew word is translated into English as "angel" from the Greek word for "messenger," *angelos*. It is the narrator who informs the reader that the three men are divine messengers; Abraham addresses them simply as "sirs." Nonetheless, he responds as a solicitous host, preparing a sumptuous meal. Abraham's care in providing for his guests underscores the importance of their message. His urgent message to Sarah may be translated, "Hurry! Three measures of choice flour. Knead and make cakes!" Abraham also instructs a servant to prepare a calf—a lavish meal is made. This hospitality provides the catalyst to involve Sarah in the promises, even though she still is never addressed directly by God.

The true purpose of the visit is announced in verse 9. Both the messengers and Abraham believe Sarah is in the tent before they specify that it is she who is to bear a child within a year. The phrase used to indicate a year's passing is unusual: *Kaet hayyah,* literally, "the time it is reviving," refers to spring. But as another use in the Hebrew Bible shows, the elderly Shunnamite woman is also promised with this phrase that she will bear a son in the following spring (2 Kings 4:16-17). The emphasis is on the rebirth of this season. It is an appropriate indicator of the role that Sarah will have in the birth of the Israelite nation. As usual, Sarah is excluded from the direct revelation—or so it seems. Unknown to Abraham or to the messengers, she is listening at the tent door. Sarah is able to take action in this scene even though her social standing is subordinate to her husband and to the (male) messengers. What she overhears comes as a shock. Reminiscent of Abraham's earlier laughter, she laughs, thus underscoring the apparent impossibility of God's plans in the estimation of the first ancestors of Israel.

A literal translation of verses 11 and 12 shows the poignancy of her plight. The narrator explains that "it had ceased to be with Sarah in the manner of women"—a reference that her periods had ended. When Sarah finally has a chance to speak in this scene, she laments, "After I am worn out, and my husband is old, shall I have pleasure?" Her statement is pregnant with meaning, referring not only to her age, but also to her exhaustion and despair. Here the narrator so well expresses the difficulty of belief when one's spirit is overwhelmed. Perhaps it is because of the reasonableness of her disbelief that she is only briefly reprimanded for her denial of her laughter when confronted by God. Even the narrator pauses to give us a reason—she laughed because she was afraid.

The next text concerning Sarah, 21:1-7, speaks of the fulfillment of God's promises. God accomplished the unexpected. Sarah's name features frequently in this short section. Here the fulfillment of the promise is put expressly in terms of granting favor to *Sarah*. It becomes clear to the reader that God's promise was not only to Abraham—not any child born to him was the one chosen by God to inherit the promise—but only the one born to Sarah. The name Isaac means laughter, recalling the laughter, equivalent to doubt, of both his parents. Now, however, laughter is associated with a new aspect of Sarah's life as she and those around her laugh joyously. The presentation of her relief and delight are completed by the reference to Isaac's weaning—he has survived the precarious period of infancy.

Sarah's life was beyond her control on so many levels and on so many occasions. She followed her husband on long and treacherous journeys. Twice she was threatened by Pharaoh and Abimelech when Abraham forced her to pretend she was his sister so that his safety would not be compromised. She suffers disgrace by the community for her long infertility and is taunted by her maid when she cannot have a child. As a member of a patriarchal society, she is below the hierarchy of men but above the class of women servants and thus participates in the cruel saga of Hagar's life. Did the narrator intend for the reader to surmise that Sarah knew about God's command to Abraham to sacrifice Isaac? Could one imagine a more painful episode for this woman? In spite of these endurance tests, God chose her to be the mother of the covenantal promise. Although Abraham and Sarah herself would have chosen another route for Abraham to have a son, God determined that no one else would take her place.

Retelling the Story

"I had really given up all hope of having children, that day those three strangers came to our tent. I was inside, tending to my household chores, so I didn't see them coming. Actually, Abraham said he'd not seen them coming, either. They just sort of materialized—three men, just standing there, at a little distance from the door of the tent.

"Perhaps he sensed there was something special about them. Or maybe it was just our Hebrew hospitality. But he rushed up to them, invited them to stay a while, to wash their feet, rest under the tree, have a little food.

"They agreed. He ran in to tell me to make some bread, and he got meat for them and some milk and butter and brought out the food and set it before them.

"They ate. No big surprises, so far.

"But then . . . I was still inside the tent—out of sight, you understand—resting after the rush to get food ready, enjoying the hum of voices, when I heard one of them say, 'Where's your wife? Sarah?'

"They knew my name! Abraham hadn't told them. I certainly hadn't. I'd done my best to keep out of their way. Even if they'd seen me, how would they know my name?

"Abraham was dumbfounded, too. But he just said, 'She's in the tent.'

"Then the one who seemed to be the leader made the most astonishing statement. In the first place, it was an odd subject to bring up about a virtual stranger. In the second place, he might have guessed that Abraham, as old as he was, would have a wife who was no spring chicken. Although, of course, lots of men do marry younger women—but *that* much younger?

"Anyway, this fellow said, 'Your wife is going to have a son.'

"*Oh, sure,* I thought. *Come on, guys.* You could have knocked me over with a feather. In the first place, it's none of a stranger's business to be speculating about the reproductive life of people he doesn't even know. And in the second place I'd passed through menopause years ago! *No way am I going to get pregnant at my age,* I thought.

> When the visitors came to see Abraham and Sarah to give them the news that they would finally be parents, Sarah prepared "cakes" of unleavened bread. The messengers did not eat the bread, however, since as they spoke and Sarah laughed, for the first time in decades Sarah began her period. This would render the bread she was baking ritually unclean. Other rabbis disagree, saying that the passage simply means that the visitors ate only unleavened bread because it was the season of Passover. The fact that the people of God had not yet entered the land of Egypt nor been redeemed from slavery does not seem to play a role in their interpretation. Perhaps that is because the cycle of the year would be celebrated by God and the heavenly host even before it entered into history. (*Genesis Rabbah* 43.14 and *Exodus Rabbah* 15.12)

24

"So I laughed to myself. Now this is important. I laughed to myself. Didn't open my mouth. Didn't make a peep. Didn't stifle a chuckle. To myself I laughed. I was inside the tent, so he couldn't even have seen a smile pass over my face.

"Well, the man was a mind reader, because he says, to Abraham, 'How come your wife laughed? She thinks she's too old to have a baby? Is anything impossible with God?'

"With God? I thought. What is this? And who is this stranger who knows my name and sees into my heart to know that I laughed—and then make the preposterous suggestion?

"This time I didn't laugh, let me tell you. I was afraid. That fellow might have thought I'd been rude, and what other power might he have? I stepped to the doorway of the tent. 'I didn't laugh,' I said, my voice trembling.

In order to keep peace between Abraham and Sarah, the messenger stretched the truth just a little. When Sarah laughed at the idea of having a child she said aloud, "But my husband is old." But when the messenger reported the conversation to Abraham, he said, "Your wife asked 'How am I to have a child? My husband is old *and I am old.' "* Thus the messenger of God kept peace in the family. (*Leviticus Rabbah* 9.9)

" 'Yes, you did.' he said. 'I'll come back again. You'll see. By the time I come back, you'll have that son.'

"They left. I was glad to see them go. But shaken, too.

"Abraham and I sat down and talked about it. Was this visitor a seer? Did he know something we didn't know? To become parents at our age?

"It had been very painful to us that we couldn't conceive a child. We'd been married young. At first I was in no hurry. I don't think he was either. We were having a lot of fun, just the two of us. Time enough for children when we were a little older, more ready to settle down.

"But we did nothing to prevent my getting pregnant, either, and after a few years we began to wonder—was there something wrong? We consulted doctors. We tried all the folk remedies. But nothing happened. After many years we gave up, resigned ourselves to childlessness, spent time with our nieces and nephews, the other children of the tribe.

"But the heartache stayed. So that, old as I was, even behind my laughter— my *silent* laughter—was a tiny leap of hope. Crazy as it seemed, could it be so? Could that stranger be right? The one who knew my name, who heard my silent laughter?"

She tips her head back and laughs, careful not to jostle the baby in her arms. "Now God has given me joy, to laugh aloud!" She holds up the baby for the visitor to see—"Look at him. Isaac," she murmurs against the baby's downy cheek. *(Martha Whitmore Hickman)*

The power of names in the ancient world is demonstrated by the sages who say that the change of Abram to Abraham and Sarai to Sarah was a radical transformation. In truth, God was saying, according to these rabbis, that while Abram could not be a father, Abraham could; and while Sarai could bear no children, Sarah would. Such is the potency of a new name given by God. (*Ecclesiastes Rabbah*, 5.6)

Hagar

After Sarah has Abraham send Hagar and Ishmael away, God saves the lives of this mother and son, and then makes a promise to them as well.

The Story

The boy grew and was weaned, and on the day of his weaning Abraham gave a great feast.

Sarah saw the son whom Hagar the Egyptian had borne to Abraham playing with Isaac, and she said to Abraham, 'Drive out this slave-girl and her son! I will not have this slave's son sharing the inheritance with my son Isaac.' Abraham was very upset at this because of Ishmael, but God said to him, 'Do not be upset for the boy and your slave-girl. Do as Sarah says, because it is through Isaac's line that your name will be perpetuated.'

Comments on the Story

The occasion of the celebration of Isaac's weaning prompts the second conflict between Sarah and Hagar. Hagar, Sarah's servant, has had a difficult life. Previously, Sarah devised the plan that Abraham would have a son through Hagar because Sarah could not conceive. Her plan had unintended consequences; Hagar's pregnancy caused rivalry between the women. This scene recalls the earlier flight of Hagar into the wilderness during her pregnancy. At that time, an angel appeared to her and promised that her son, Ishmael (meaning "God hears"), would be the father of a great nation. By casting this scene in a similar location, parallels are easily drawn in the reader's mind. God's messenger responded to Hagar before—will God respond again? Hagar returned to Sarah in the past—will she again? God told Hagar that Ishmael would be a man who would struggle against others. Is the conflict between Hagar and Sarah an indication of the beginning of these troubles?

In the context of the Abraham cycle, it is clear that Sarah's rivalry is not a simplistic case of jealousy over the prospect of sharing Abraham's wealth with another woman's child, but must be seen in the context of the covenantal promises to Israel through Abraham. The previous chapters have reiterat-

27

ed that the promises to Abraham for land, descendants, and blessing were to be inherited by his son Isaac, and Sarah had a crucial role as the carrier of the covenant by giving birth to this son. Sarah is reminded of Ishmael's threat as the father of a rival people. Therefore, she instructs Abraham to demand that Ishmael and Hagar depart from them permanently, yet Abraham hesitates. It is in this context of the separation of two peoples, therefore, that we must understand God's words to Abraham. Although God does not promise a covenant to Hagar's offspring, God nonetheless assures Abraham that the child will be the father of a great people because of his connection to Abraham.

The narrator tells the reader of the necessity of the separation by using God's own words, which add legitimacy to the harsh message. In spite of God's assurance, however, God's promise of Ishmael's well-being and future progeny seem in doubt as Hagar begins her journey. Her plight is real. She wanders about *(wateta)* in harsh territory. The word choice for "wander about" underscores her suffering and displacement. As an act of despair, she abandons her child under a bush *(siâh)* a word whose homonym means "lamentation." In a moving scene, she weeps for her son. It is interesting that Hagar refers to Ishmael as her child, emphasizing his helplessness, but when God begins to speak of him, he is called a youth, thus connoting his strength.

Although Ishmael's name is not used in this scene, the parallels with the account of Hagar in the wilderness wherein the boy's name was given by God remind the reader of the name's appropriate meaning: "God hears." An angel of God specifies to Hagar that God hears the boy crying. The promise that he will father a great nation is reiterated, and God enables Hagar to see a well. The narrator points out that God's involvement with Ishmael is not a singular occurrence; rather, God continues to be with Ishmael as he grows. The reference to Ishmael's later facility with the bow contrasts with the description that his mother placed him a bowshot away when she thought his life threatened. Ishmael becomes a man of strength. God's promise concerning Ishmael's own progeny and nation now is assured. He lives in the land of Paran, near Shur, where Hagar fled when threatened by Sarah. This territory is distinct from what will become Israel.

Although Hagar's reward is received indirectly through her son, she still acts on her own behalf. She is the only woman in the Hebrew Bible to select a wife for her son, and the woman she chooses is from Egypt, the land of her own people. Thus the narrator ends this story as it began, with an indication of the bonds between neighboring nations, and yet also with an accounting for the struggle between Israel and a rival people. Is Israel like its neighbor, the Ishmaelites, who at certain times were its enemy? Indeed, they share the same father. Because of this sensitivity the narrator can write poignantly about

Hagar's plight and about God's revelation and promise to her. Nonetheless, the two peoples are distinct—they do not both share in the covenant that God made with Abraham. They have different mothers.

Retelling the Story

The child stood at the chain link fence surrounding the great estate. Inside, a birthday party was going on—clowns and balloons and even an imported calliope and an ice cream truck with cones and sprinkles in all the flavors you could imagine. Children in party clothes ran around the lawn, rolling hoops or chasing soap bubbles, or sat on a bench eating ice cream. Tables of grown ups sprinkled the lawn, too—parents and friends of Andrew, the birthday child.

Sammy, outside the fence, his nose pressed against the twisted metal, turned to his mother, who had just come from work, her face smeared with soot from the factory where she worked, standing on her feet all day amid choking dust.

"Will my father ever invite me to a party?" the boy asked.

"Don't count on it, Sammy," his mother said. "You're a bit old for balloons and soap bubbles, aren't you?"

"I could have a swimming party—invite my friends to swim in his pool. Anyway, I was little once. He never had this kind of party for me then, either."

"Hah!" His mother pushed strands of black hair behind her ear. "We're lucky he gives us a little money from time to time. He wouldn't even do that— pay child support—if I hadn't threatened him with the law."

Sammy pointed to a woman in a long, flowered dress who was smoothing Andrew's hair. "Andrew's mother—how come she looks so cross if she ever sees us on the street?"

"We remind her of what she'd rather forget."

"What's that?"

"How your father loved me once. That for twenty years she couldn't have kids. When she finally did have Andrew, your father . . . " She stopped and sneered in the direction of the portly man lying back in a lounge chair." . . . dropped me like a hot potato. Now his world was at last complete. Hers, too. That boy has had everything—nursemaids, every toy you could imagine, even his own pony to ride. You can watch his father playing with him by the hour."

Sam, who was ten and tried never ever to cry, sniffed and brushed a sleeve across his nose. "I was here the whole time. He could have played with me."

His mother snorted. "She wouldn't allow it. She'd have banished us from the city if she could. As it was she made him chase us out of that dump of a servant's quarters. He pulled some strings to get us in public housing. He did that for you. He doesn't care about me—only that I'm somebody to take care of you. Sure as hell she wouldn't. She was furious when we got in that unit over there," she gestured across a park, "so we pass their house every day."

> When Hagar called out to God to spare her life and that of her son, Ishmael, after they had been driven from the household of Abraham and Sarah, God caused a well to appear to provide for this mother and child. One of God's angels asked why God would act with such compassion for Ishmael and Hagar when God and all the angels knew that the Ishmaelites would one day attempt to deny water to the children of Israel. God explained that divine justice is not based on what someone will do someday. Rather, each need is met based on who the person is at the time. The child was thirsty, and the mother worried, so the well was given. (*Exodus Rabbah*, 3.2)

Some dogs bounded up to the fence, and Sam put his hand out to let the dogs lick it.

"Here, Rego. Come here!" ordered a harsh voice. It was Andrew's mother. "Get away from there." She turned to a woman beside her. "Street people!" she said.

Sam's mother stepped back. "If I'm not here she won't raise such a fuss. She likes to see me even less than she likes to see you."

"Why doesn't she like to see me?" Sam rubbed his eyes, fighting tears.

"She's afraid you'll latch on to your father's money. That he'll weaken and leave you part of his estate. She wants everything for herself—and for Andrew."

"But he's my father, too." Now Sam was crying.

> Hagar was not willing to see her child die, and so she sat "some way off, about a bow shot distance." The rabbis say that the distance was considerably greater. They contend that the phrase here means that she sat a mile away. Why so far? Perhaps she could still hear her child crying for her, and a mile would have reduced even the loudest screams to silence. According to the sages, not only was Hagar unwilling to see her child die but she was unwilling to hear his death cries as well. Fortunately, she had to do neither. (*Numbers Rabbah*, 2.9)

His mother couldn't bear to see his tears. "I'm going on home," she said. "Come when you're ready."

She moved to walk along the fence enclosing the estate. At the gate she paused, looked in at the ice cream man—who waved—then, sadly, crossed the park and went home.

She didn't know, until Sam cam running to tell her, that soon after she left, the ice cream truck had rolled out of the big driveway and the driver, seeing him standing crying by the fence, had stopped and given him a triple decker—and a fistful of coupons for free ice cream, enough to last him the whole summer long. *(Martha Whitmore Hickman)*

Rebekah

Rebekah marries Isaac, gives birth to the combative twins, Jacob and Esau, then assists the younger in getting his father's blessing from the elder.

The Story

Abraham was by now a very old man, and the LORD had blessed him in all that he did. Abraham said to the servant who had been longest in his service and was in charge of all he owned, 'Give me your solemn oath: I want you to swear by the LORD, the God of heaven and earth, that you will not take a wife for my son from the women of the Canaanites among whom I am living. You must go to my own country and to my own kindred to find a wife for my son Isaac.' 'What if the woman is unwilling to come with me to this country?' the servant asked. 'Must I take your son back to the land you came from?' Abraham said to him, 'On no account are you to take my son back there. The LORD the God of heaven who took me from my father's house and the land of my birth, the LORD who swore to me that he would give this land to my descendants—he will send his angel before you, and you will take a wife from there for my son. If the woman is unwilling to come with you, then you will be released from your oath to me; only you must not take my son back there.'

The servant then put his hand under his master Abraham's thigh and swore that oath.

The servant chose ten camels from his master's herds and, with all kinds of gifts from his master, he went to Aram-naharaim, to the town where Nahor lived. Towards evening, the time when the women go out to draw water, he made the camels kneel down by the well outside the town. 'LORD God of my master Abraham,' he said, 'give me good fortune this day; keep faith with my master Abraham. Here I am by the spring, as the women of the town come out to draw water. I shall say to a girl, "Please lower your jar so that I may drink"; and if she answers, "Drink, and I shall water your camels also," let that be the girl whom you intend for your servant Isaac. In this way I shall know that you have kept faith with my master.'

Before he had finished praying, he saw Rebecca coming out with her waterjar on her shoulder. She was the daughter of Bethuel son of Milcah, the wife of Abraham's brother Nahor. The girl was very beautiful and a virgin guiltless of intercourse with any man. She went down to the spring, filled her jar, and came up again. Abraham's servant hurried to meet her and said, 'Will you give me a little water from your

33

jar?' 'Please drink, sir,' she answered, and at once lowered her jar on to her hand to let him drink. When she had finished giving him a drink, she said, 'I shall draw water for your camels also until they have had enough.' She quickly emptied her jar into the water trough, and then hurrying again to the well she drew water and watered all the camels.

The man was watching quietly to see whether or not the LORD had made his journey successful, and when the camels had finished drinking, he took a gold nose-ring weighing half a shekel, and two bracelets for her wrists weighing ten shekels, also of gold. 'Tell me, please, whose daughter you are,' he said. 'Is there room in your father's house for us to spend the night?' She answered, 'I am the daughter of Bethuel son of Nahor and Milcah; we have plenty of straw and fodder and also room for you to spend the night.' So the man bowed down and prostrated himself before the LORD and said, 'Blessed be the LORD the God of my master Abraham. His faithfulness to my master has been constant and unfailing, for he has guided me to the house of my master's kinsman.' . . .

When they rose in the morning, Abraham's servant said, 'Give me leave to go back to my master.' Rebecca's brother and her mother replied, 'Let the girl stay with us for a few days, say ten days, and then she can go.' But he said to them, 'Do not detain me, for it is the LORD who has granted me success. Give me leave to go back to my master.' They said, 'Let us call the girl and see what she says.' They called Rebecca and asked her if she would go with the man, and she answered, 'Yes, I will go.' So they let their sister Rebecca and her maid go with Abraham's servant

and his men. They blessed Rebecca and said to her:

'You are our sister, may you be the
   mother of many children;
may your sons possess the cities of
   their enemies.'

Rebecca and her companions mounted their camels to follow the man. So the servant took Rebecca and set out.

Isaac meanwhile had moved on as far as Beer-lahai-roi and was living in the Negeb. One evening when he had gone out into the open country hoping to meet them, he looked and saw camels approaching. When Rebecca saw Isaac, she dismounted from her camel, saying to the servant, 'Who is that man walking across the open country toward us?' When the servant answered, 'It is my master,' she took her veil and covered herself. The servant related to Isaac all that had happened. Isaac conducted her into the tent and took her as his wife. So she became his wife, and he loved her and was consoled for the death of his mother.

This is an account of the descendants of Abraham's son Isaac. Isaac's father was Abraham. When Isaac was forty years old he married Rebecca daughter of Bethuel, the Aramaean from Paddan-aram and sister of Laban the Aramaean. Isaac appealed to the LORD on behalf of his wife because she was childless; the LORD gave heed to his entreaty, and Rebecca conceived. The children pressed on each other in her womb, and she said, "If all is well, why am I like this?" She went to seek guidance of the LORD, who said to her:

'Two nations are in your womb,
two peoples going their own ways
   from birth.
One will be stronger than the other;

the elder will be servant to the younger.'

Then his father said to him, 'Come near, my son, and kiss me.' So he went near and kissed him, and when Isaac smelt the smell of his clothes, he blessed him and said, 'The smell of my son is like the smell of open country blessed by the LORD.

When Isaac grew old and his eyes had become so dim that he could not see, he called for his elder son Esau. 'My son!' he said. Esau answered, 'Here I am.' Isaac said, 'Listen now: I am old and I do not know when I may die. Take your hunting gear, your quiver and bow, and go out into the country and get me some game. Then make me a savoury dish, the kind I like, and bring it for me to eat so that I may give you my blessing before I die.'

Now Rebecca had been listening as Isaac talked to his son Esau. When Esau went off into the country to hunt game for his father, she said to her son Jacob, 'I have just overheard your father say to your brother Esau, "Bring me some game and make a savoury dish for me to eat so that I may bless you in the presence of the LORD before I die." Listen now to me, my son, and do what I tell you. Go to the flock and pick me out two fine young kids, and I shall make them into a savoury dish for your

father, the kind he likes. Then take it in to your father to eat so that he may bless you before he dies.' 'But my brother Esau is a hairy man,' Jacob said to his mother Rebecca, 'and my skin is smooth. Suppose my father touches me; he will know that I am playing a trick on him and I shall bring a curse instead of a blessing on myself.' His mother answered, 'Let any curse for you fall on me, my son. Do as I say; go and fetch me the kids.' So Jacob went and got them and brought them to his mother, who made them into a savoury dish such as his father liked. Rebecca then took her elder son's clothes, Esau's best clothes which she had by her in the house, and put them on Jacob her younger son. She put the goatskins on his hands and on the smooth nape of his neck. Then she handed to her son Jacob the savoury dish and the bread she had made.
'God give you dew from heaven
and the richness of the earth,
corn and new wine in plenty!
May peoples serve you
and nations bow down to you.
May you be lord over your brothers,
and may your mother's sons bow
   down to you.
A curse on those who curse you,
but a blessing on those who bless
   you!'

Comments on the Story

At this point in the narrative about the ancestors of Israel, the account of the first generation (Abraham and Sarah) is about to end. Sarah is dead, and Abraham is old. Isaac, the sole inheritor of God's covenantal promise to Abraham, is without a wife; thus the continuation of the people of the promise is in doubt. Finding the proper wife for Isaac is now crucial. Abraham acts by sending his most trusted servant to the land of his ancestors to find Isaac a wife. The concern to find a woman from his native land does not stem from a fear of foreigners per se, but points to the problem of finding someone willing to fol-

35

low in the covenantal ways of God. Abraham is adamant that his son not return to his ancestral land. The servant is not to agree to a marriage if the woman is unwilling to return with him. For the audience of the final version of this text, who experienced exile in Babylon, the importance of the promise of the land of Canaan is highlighted.

God's involvement in the selection of Rebekah as a mother of Israel is indicated in several ways. Not only does Abraham indicate to the servant that God will guide him, but the servant prays for a sign as well. Indeed, the first woman he meets is Rebekah. The location at the well is significant because the ancient reader would associate well scenes with betrothals (as occurs with Jacob and Rachel and with Moses and Zipporah). The narrator indicates that Rebekah is the chosen one by her description. She is Abraham's kin, thus appropriate for the faith; a virgin, therefore suitable as a wife; and beautiful, an indication of fertility. Her individuality and character are developed by the description of her interaction with the servant. In her generosity she offers to give water not only to him but to all of his camels as well, even though the servant has ten camels and she has only one jar.

Although the servant's encounter with Rebekah happened serendipitously, the narrator still underscores the necessity of God's providence in this text. Various things happen that jeopardize the success of the servant's journey. The servant offers Rebekah all of Abraham's gifts before he is certain of her identity and status. Later, her family asks for a delay. As an indication of Rebekah's forthrightness, she solves the problem. Speaking unequivocally, she states, "Yes, I will go" (v. 50). Will her family approve? Fortunately, they respond with a blessing and refer to her future descendants. The journey back to Isaac transpires safely, and when Isaac sees her they immediately become husband and wife, thereby stressing the importance of having descendants. The reference to Isaac's being comforted after his mother's death confirms that the thrust of the narrative now shifts to the second generation.

Just as Sarah was infertile, so too is Rebekah. The depictions of infertile women in the Hebrew Bible are often used to highlight the intervention of God and the subsequent birth of a son who has an ordained purpose in God's plan for Israel. Faced with a troublesome pregnancy, Rebekah prays to God, who answers her directly! The use of poetry for God's words highlights their significance. The message she gets is striking: Not only will she bear twins, but the older will be of lesser status. It will be the secondborn, Jacob, who will receive the covenantal blessing, although the normal expectation would be that the firstborn, Esau, receive it. A parallel may be drawn to the first generation of Israel's ancestors. Isaac, Abraham's secondborn, actually received the rights of primogeniture. Thus, by "breaking the rules," God's providential care and plan are emphasized.

Another parallel of Rebekah to Sarah is drawn in the next scene. Just as Sarah received crucial information about her role in actualizing the covenant by overhearing it at the tent door, so too does Rebekah overhear that Isaac will designate Esau to receive his blessing. Yet she, and not Isaac, knows of God's choice of Jacob. Thus she must take action, but because of her lesser authority, she must act deceptively. Frequently, deception is a category of action used by persons in the Hebrew Bible who are powerless against authority figures. Rachel, for example, uses deception when her life is threatened by Laban, and Jacob uses deception when treated unfairly by the stronger Laban. Whereas some modern commentators see Rebekah as manipulative of the weakened Isaac or unfair to Esau, the context of God's revelation to her shows that she is acting appropriately. Her plan is brilliant, and it succeeds. She disarms Jacob of his fear of reprisal by taking on the consequences of any curse and prepares not only the food but also the clothing to enable Jacob to feel and smell like Esau to the blind Isaac. God's plan for the second generation is fulfilled when we hear the words of blessing from Isaac. It includes fertility of the land, strength among foreigners, and many descendants. God's promise to the first generation has been beset by obstacles, but it continues to be fulfilled.

In this account of Rebekah and Isaac, Rebekah challenges the prevailing wisdom. She, not Isaac, receives a direct message from God concerning the births and roles of her sons. She determines that Isaac bless the properly designated child. And by ensuring Jacob's escape when Esau threatens him, she continues in her dual role to protect him and the future of her people.

Retelling the Story

It was long ago, an ordinary evening in my village of Haran. I had gone with the other women to draw water at the well. At first I scarcely noticed the stranger there with his kneeling camels. He appeared to be waiting for something. I saw him watching me, and when I had filled my jar and was returning from the well, he came and asked me for drink. I could tell he had come from far away. Of course, I gave him water. Then I said, "Your camels are thirty too. Let me get water for them." So I did. All the while he was giving me this strange look, studying my face.

His name was Eliezer, servant of Abraham, and as it turned out, he and his men spent the night at our place. He told us he was searching for a wife for his master, Isaac. He felt the Lord had led him to me!

In the morning he wanted to take me to Isaac, right away.

My mother and brother demurred. "Wait ten days," they begged. "It's too soon for us to let her go."

Rebekah was a woman even the forces of nature respected. The sages say that when she went to draw water from a well she did not have to bend far over and reach into its depths to fill her water jar. Rather, the level of the water would rise so she could fill her container with ease. (*Genesis Rabbah* 60.5)

But Eliezer said, "She's the one I've been sent to find. Don't hold me back. My master is waiting."

They turned to me. "You decide. Will you go with this man?"

I said, "Yes, I will go." It was a rash thing to do, but my heart told me it was right.

My family gave me their blessing, and I set forth for the land of Canaan and for my marriage to a man I had never met.

But ah! when I saw him coming, I stepped down from my camel and covered myself with a veil. Isaac came to meet me, and there was love in his eyes as he brought me to his tent, and I became his wife.

For a long time I did not conceive. When I did, the pregnancy was so hard I wished I were dead. Then the Lord said to me, "The twins you are carrying will be adversaries. Already they fight within you." And then this: "The one who is older will serve the one who is younger." I did not tell Isaac what I had heard.

In due time the twins were born. First, Esau, then Jacob. Esau grew to be a hunter, a man of action, a sometimes violent man—a stranger to me. And Jacob—my thoughtful, sensitive younger son, who stayed home, spent long hours with me—Jacob, my beloved.

When my Isaac grew old and all but blind and knew he couldn't live much longer, he called Esau to his side and said, "You are the elder. The birthright belongs to you. Go out to the field and hunt game, and make my favorite stew and bring it to me to eat, that I may bless you before I die." And Esau went off to do as his father said.

But I had overheard my husband.

I summoned my Jacob to me.

"Hurry. Bring me two young lambs. I'll make the stew your father wants. You offer it to him. He can't see. He'll give the blessing to you."

Jacob was skeptical and timid. "It'll never work. I'm virtually beardless. I have no hair on my neck and arms. My father will touch me, and he'll curse me for a fraud."

"Trust me," I said, "We'll dress you in Esau's clothes, so the smell of your brother will be on you. I'll lay the furry skin of the lambs on your forearms and your neck. Your father will be fooled. He'll think you are your brother. He'll give the blessing to you."

So Jacob killed the lambs, and I made the stew. We dressed Jacob in his brother's clothes. I put the skin of the lambs on his arms and on his neck. Then, trembling, I sent him in to his father.

38

Then I stood by the door, anxious lest Esau return too soon.
And I listened while Isaac gave Jacob the birthright.
(Martha Whitmore Hickman)

> While the Bible is very specific about the burial places of the early ancestors of Israel, it does not specify the place where Rebekah was buried. Some say that this was because there was no one still alive who was worthy of preceding her body in the burial procession. Abraham and Isaac were dead, Jacob had moved away, and Esau was not worthy to precede his mother to her tomb. So she was taken out to a secret place and buried at night. (*Sefer Ha-Aggadah,* 50.87)

• • •

A mutual friend had introduced them—someone from Jim's hometown who met Susan on a trip he'd taken back to the East. It wasn't hard for him to persuade Susan to apply for a teaching job in South Dakota. It still had some frontier aspects, and teaching jobs were hard to find in the overpopulated East. "When you come," the friend said, "I want you to meet Jim Moody."

> The story of Rebekah was remembered down the centuries by young women who came to the wells and were from time to time asked to serve strangers. One girl approached the well in her village when a man she had never seen before asked her for a drink. When he had quenched his thirst, he asked for his donkey to be given a drink. The girl complied. As the stranger turned to go without offering anything to the girl for her trouble, he said, "You, young lady, have acted like Rebekah." Remembering that Abraham's servant had given a gold nose ring and two gold bracelets to her ancestor, the girl replied, "True, sir, but you have not acted like Eliezer." (*Lamentations Rabbah* 1.1 (19))

The first time Jim and Susan met—it was a community picnic on the Fourth of July—it was love at first sight, and by the time the sky was showered with fireworks of rockets and falling stars, there were stars in their eyes as well.

She wrote home and told her folks—who'd been reluctant to see her go—that the job was working out. She had fallen in love, and this was where she wanted to make her home.

Her family was a little taken aback that it had all happened so suddenly; they would have liked time to arrange a big wedding. But neither Susan nor Jim wanted to wait, so they were married right away, and for a while everything seemed wonderful.

39

They wanted children, and for a long time Susan didn't get pregnant. But after her first dose of fertility drugs, she did—with twins.

The pregnancy was hard. The twins were very active early in the pregnancy; the morning sickness lasted six months. She had headaches, and her feet swelled. She said to Jim, only half-jokingly, "I'm not sure it's worth it. Plus, these kids are so agitated. I have this image of them duking it out in the womb!" It was in the days before ultrasound, so she didn't know whether they were girls or boys, or one of each.

They turned out to be two girls, but you could scarcely imagine two children more different from each other. The firstborn, Samantha, was a tomboy. She loved baseball and soccer and racing. She was a large child, strong, well-coordinated, and she rather dominated her younger, frailer sister—the secondborn, whom they named Serena, after a favorite aunt of Susan's. Not only were the girls different in nature and physique, but they didn't get along with each other. Not at all. They fought all the time. Jim tended to favor Samantha, or Sam, as she came to be called. He was a lover of sports, and so was she, and when she became, in college, a star basketball player he traveled around the country following the team, so he could watch her play.

> By meeting her husband-to-be at a well, Rebekah began a family tradition. The sages say that not only did her son Jacob meet his beloved Rachel at a well, but Moses met his future wife when he sat down at a well in Midian and the daughters of Jethro, priest of Midian, came to draw water. For the rabbis, meeting a future spouse at a well became an act that continued the traditions of their ancestors, but also indicated the purity of the union. (*Exodus Rabbah* 1.32)

> When Isaac marries Rebekah, she is referred to as "daughter of Bethuel, the Aramean from Paddan-aram and sister of Laban the Aramean." Many of us today assume that such references are a result of a patriarchal society in which women had no real identity except in their relations to fathers, brothers, and husbands. But the rabbis took another approach to the phrasing of Rebekah's introduction. They say that her father and brother are both mentioned in such a fashion that the reader is warned that they are tricksters and not to be trusted. These sages suggest that the remarkable thing in this passage is that a spirit as pure as Rebekah's could come from such a suspect family. Still, we may wish to remember these roots when she begins to advance the prospects of her younger (and favorite) son, Jacob, over the traditional familial rights of his brother, Esau. (*Leviticus Rabbah* 23.1)

Serena, on the other hand, was a dainty, ladylike child and woman. She loved domestic things—loved to help Susan in the kitchen, was always scheming for new ways to improve the modest house they lived in, and always took particular interest in things Sarah loved, too—especially some family heirlooms, which they all jokingly referred to as "The Inheritance"—pieces of silver, some family jewelry, a quite valuable collection of gold pieces that had somehow escaped the government's commandeering of gold—all of which had come down through Jim's family and was languishing in the family's safe deposit box at the bank.

Time passed. Each of the girls married, had children of her own. Sam continued to be her father's favorite; Serena, her mother's.

As Jim's eyesight began to fail and Susan was having more and more trouble with arthritis, they did what they should have done long before—engaged a lawyer to help them make out their wills.

"We'll divide our property more or less evenly, right?" Jim asked. "Although I'd like that stuff that came down through my family to go to Sam."

"More or less evenly," Susan agreed, but in her head she thought, "We'll see," because she wanted the family heirlooms to go to Serena.

The wills were made out according to Jim's wish. In a way, it was his to dispose of.

One afternoon, when both girls had come from out of town to visit their parents, and Jim and Samantha had gone off fishing, Susan and Serena went back to the lawyer's office and had him make a new will, giving the treasure to Serena.

"Dad will never sign this," Serena said.

"He won't see it," her mother said. "He won't be able to read it, his eyes are so bad."

After a few days, the girls returned to their homes and Susan and Jim went in for the final signing of the will.

The lawyer handed them each a copy. "Please read this over carefully," he said.

Susan held her breath, watching as Jim, brow furrowed over his thick glasses, began to study the pages. After a minute or two he handed the document to the lawyer. "Such small print," he said. "But it's fine. I know it's fine."

Then they each signed the copies of the will and put them in the safe deposit box, along with the silver, the jewelry, and the collection of gold coins. *(Martha Whitmore Hickman)*

Rachel

Rachel, Jacob's beloved for whose hand in marriage he had worked fourteen years, finally gives birth to a child, Joseph, and with her sister and husband leaves her father's house.

The Story

Laban said to him, 'Why should you work for me for nothing simply because you are my kinsman? Tell me what wage you would settle for.' Now Laban had two daughters: the elder was called Leah, and the younger Rachel. Leah was dull-eyed, but Rachel was beautiful in both face and figure, and Jacob had fallen in love with her. He said, 'For your younger daughter Rachel I would work seven years.' Laban replied, 'It is better that I should give her to you than to anyone else; stay with me.'

When Jacob had worked seven years for Rachel, and they seemed like a few days because he loved her, her said to Laban, 'I have served my time. Give me my wife that I may lie with her.' Laban brought all the people of the place together and held a wedding feast. In the evening he took his daughter Leah and brought her to Jacob, and he lay with her. At the same time Laban gave his slave-girl Zilpah to his daughter Leah. But when morning came, there was Leah! Jacob said to Laban, 'What is this you have done to me? It was for Rachel I worked. Why have you played this trick on me?' Laban answered, 'It is against the custom of our country to

marry off the younger sister before the elder. Go through with the seven days' feast for the elder, and the younger shall be given you in return for a further seven years' work.' Jacob agreed, and completed the seven days for Leah.

Then Laban gave Jacob his daughter Rachel to be his wife; and to serve Rachel he gave his slave-girl Bilhah. Jacob lay with Rachel also; he loved her rather than Leah, and he worked for Laban for a further seven years. When the LORD saw that Leah was unloved, he granted her a child, but Rachel remained childless. Leah conceived and gave birth to a son; and she called him Reuben, for she said, "The LORD has seen my humiliation, but now my husband will love me.' Again she conceived and had a son and said, 'The LORD, hearing that I am unloved, has given me this child also'; and she called him Simeon. She conceived again and had a son and said, 'Now that I have borne him three sons my husband will surely be attached to me.' So she called him Levi. Once more she conceived and had a son, and said, 'Now I shall praise the LORD'; therefore she named him Judah. Then for a while she bore no more children. . . .

Then God took thought for Rachel; he heard her prayer and gave her a child. After she conceived and bore a son, she said, 'God has taken away my humiliation.' She named him Joseph, saying, 'May the Lord add another son to me!'. . .

Jacob learnt that Laban's sons were saying, 'Jacob has taken everything that our father had, and all his wealth has come from our father's property.' He noticed also that Laban was not so well disposed to him as he had once been. The LORD said to Jacob, 'Go back to the land of your fathers and to your kindred; I shall be with you,' and Jacob sent word to Rachel and Leah to come out to where his flocks were in the country. He said to them, 'I have been noticing that your father is not so friendly to me as once he was. But the God of my father has been with me. You yourselves know I have served your father to the best of my ability, yet he has cheated me and changed my wages ten times over. But God did not let him do me any harm. . . . Rachel and Leah answered him, 'We no longer have any share in our father's house. Does he not look on us as strangers, now that he has sold us and used the money paid for us? All the wealth which God has saved from our father's clutches is surely ours and our children's. Now do whatever God has told you to do.'

Comments on the Story

Jacob arrives from Canaan to find a wife from Abraham's ancestral land, paralleling the journey of Abraham's servant to find a wife for Isaac. The narrator thus emphasizes the need to find a wife who will follow the covenantal tradition. Here the narrator's concerns for his or her present-day audience is apparent: Jews should avoid marrying those outside their faith to remain loyal to God and God's commandments.

Jacob finds his beloved—Rachel—a woman of Abraham's kin. Her beauty attracts him and sets the stage for the upcoming plot: Laban's deception, the suffering of Leah, and the ironic infertility of Rachel. In addition, Laban's deception prepares for the birth of the eponymous ancestors of the twelve tribes of Israel.* Jacob will marry two wives, who, along with their two servants, become the mothers of Jacob's twelve sons. Indeed, the women's names are indicative of their maternal importance. Leah means "cow" and Rachel "ewe," animals associated with fertility.

Although the ultimate outcome of Laban's deception will be for the good of Israel, his characterization is cast in a negative light. He acts solely for his own gain. Avoiding the responsibility of the father to find a husband for his firstborn, Leah, he tricks Jacob into marrying her. His excuse that the firstborn must be wed before the secondborn rings hollow, because he had

---

*Jacobs's sons' (and later, grandsons') names comprise the sources for the names of the tribes of Israel.

previously consented to the marriage of Rachel and remained silent about the custom when it would have been appropriate to speak. Laban, moreover, benefits by having Jacob work another seven years in order to marry Rachel.

Sadly, this deception has not only denied Rachel the possibility of being the single beloved wife of Jacob, but causes Leah great suffering. Forced into a marriage that Jacob did not want, it is no surprise that he makes obvious his preferred love for Rachel. In these dire circumstances, God responds to her by giving her children. The poignancy of her plight is indicated by the names she gives her first four sons. "Reuben" is a play on words with the word *see* in the phrase, "the LORD has seen my humiliation" (29:32). "Simeon" is a play on words with the word *hear* in the phrase "the LORD, hearing I am unloved has given me this child also" (29:33). Similarly, "Levi," meaning "join," corresponds to the phrase "my husband will surely be attached to me" (29:34). The name of her fourth son, however, brings the reader back to Leah's plight. In naming Judah she states, "Now I shall praise the LORD" (29:35), suggesting the futility of her quest to have Jacob love her.

In contrast to the less attractive sister who is fertile, the beautiful Rachel remains unable to have a child. After expressing her suffering to an unsympathetic husband (30:1-2), Rachel tells Jacob to have intercourse with her maid Bilhah, by whom he has Dan and Naphtali. Leah responds similarly, having Jacob lie with her servant Zilpah, who gives birth to Gad and Asher. The absence of conflict or moral judgment about these surrogate relationships suggests that it may have been an acceptable practice at some point in Israel's experience. It is interesting to note that although marriage with more than one woman was permissible, marriage to two sisters was outlawed. The narrator's audience would not have understood Jacob to be committing a sin by having both Leah and Rachel as wives, however, because the literary setting occurs before the giving of the Torah to Moses.

As Rachel continues childless she tries to gain control over her plight by bargaining to use the mandrakes that Leah had obtained from her son Reuben. By using this fertility plant, also considered to be an aphrodisiac, Rachel hopes that the next time she lies with Jacob she will become pregnant. In contrast to human initiative, however, the narrator makes clear that God is still involved in allowing these women to conceive. The use of irony continues, for Leah gives birth to Issachar, Zebulun, and Dinah without the benefit of the mandrakes. Rachel finally conceives, not because she has the fertility plant, but because God listens to her plight and enables Joseph to be born.

Biblical historians make clear that the origins of Israel's tribes are much more complex than the literary picture presented here, stemming from the inclusion of smaller groups, both native to and from outside Canaan. By incorporating this literary history, the narrator emphasizes the relationships among

45

the tribes as Israel experienced them throughout their history and memory. All Israelites are related, yet the diversity in their relationships as tribes can be partly explained by their origins from different mothers.

Once all the children are born, the covenantal promise of descendants appears intact, and the crucial roles of Rachel and Leah as key ancestresses of Israel are apparent. Like Sarah and Rebekah before them, their role in the fulfillment of the covenant is not ancillary. While it is true that these women reflect a patriarchal goal of their society in wanting to have sons, nonetheless their personal joy and fulfillment are noted when they give birth. In addition, their importance for the covenant does not end with their childbearing. When Laban cheats Jacob of his wages he unwittingly sets the stage for Jacob and his family's return to Canaan. At this moment Rachel and Leah have a crucial role in seeing that the eponymous ancestors of the twelve tribes of Israel locate in the land of God's covenantal promise. When Jacob explains Laban's treachery to them, they speak in a unified voice. In spite of their jealousy of each other, which was caused in part by their father's schemes, they both assert their independence in their decision to break with Laban. They agree to move their families to Canaan. After this development, we read no more of their jealousy. Rachel and Leah make possible the future life of their people in the land of the promise—Israel.

Retelling the Story

I am the older sister. I'm not the pretty one—ever since I've been a child I've had this cast in my eye. My father has made repeated attempts to marry me off. But no takers. They all greeted me nicely, but they looked past me to her. I pretended not to notice, tried to interest myself in other things. I love children. I worked in orphanages, tried to fill my life with worthwhile activities and forget I was the one no one wanted.

From the first time they met, Jacob loved Rachel with a special affection. After working for her father, Laban, for seven years, then being tricked into marrying Leah, he worked an additional seven years for the privilege of Rachel's companionship in marriage. Of the years he worked for Rachel's hand in marriage, Genesis says, "They seemed like a few days because he loved her." The rabbis say that when Rachel died Jacob said that of the many terrible things that had happened to him during his life the death of his beloved Rachel was by far the worst. (*Ruth Rabbah*, 2.7)

Then he came, our handsome cousin, looking to settle in our part of the country, looking for a job and a wife.

46

My father realized that this might be the opportunity he'd waited for—though none of us knew just how far he'd go to get his millstone (me) off his neck.

"Work for me, Jacob. But just because you're my relative, no reason you should work for free. What would you like for pay?" He asked this, mind you, when Rachel was nearby, tending her garden.

It didn't take Jacob long to rise to the bait. "I'll work for nothing for seven years," he offered, "if at the end of that time you'll give me Rachel as my wife." (Jealous though I am of my sister, it galls me that no one asked her how she felt about this bargain. But that's the way in our land. Women have no say—as I was to find out later when I was forced into the fraudulent scheme.)

"It's a deal," my father said. Even then I suspect the wheels were turning in his head.

Seven years went by. Jacob worked with us, lived with us. I watched him, how his eyes turned always to my sister.

At the end of the time he came to my father. "I have worked my seven years. Now give me Rachel as my wife."

"Fair enough," my father said, and set about to prepare for the week of wedding feasting.

But on the night of the wedding, the first night of the week, which was to have been Rachel and Jacob's nuptial night, when everyone was a little high on the feasting, my father insisted that I get into the marriage bed instead of Rachel.

"Father!" I said. "He wants Rachel. Do you think he won't know? He'll be furious—may come to blows with you!" In my heart I cringed at the thought of being made love to by a man who didn't want me, who thought I was someone else. But no use appealing to my father on that score.

"Honey," he said, pulling me along. "In the dark, how can he tell? I'll handle it. Don't worry."

I went. I had no choice. When Jacob slipped into the bed, I said no word. When he came to me, I received him. Then I turned away, buried my face in the bed cushions so he could not hear me cry.

Jacob slept soundly, snoring away. I didn't sleep a wink. In the morning my husband, this man who had taken my virginity, leaned tenderly against my shoulder, and then saw my face.

His own face contorted. "You are Leah!" he rasped.

"I am Leah," I said, trying to keep my voice steady, though I was cowering beneath the coverlet. "My father. It's my father's doing. Speak to him."

He stormed from the room, and I buried my head and sobbed out my silent scream. "Why am I chosen to be the ugly one, the one no one wants?"

Well, he made a deal with my father. If Jacob would stay with the festivities, the charade, for the week, then he would have Rachel as well—for another seven years of free labor.

So now Rachel and I are married to the same man. I love him, too—in spite of our terrible beginning. For a long time Rachel had no children. I bore him children—four strong sons. Each time I hoped this would earn my husband's love. Then, finally, Rachel had Joseph, so I lost the single advantage that I had.

In spite of his great love for Rachel, say the sages, Jacob was responsible for her death. After Jacob, Rachel, Leah, and their entourage had left Laban's house, the household gods were discovered to be missing. When Laban caught up with his daughters and son-in-law, he demanded to have his possessions returned. Having no knowledge that Rachel had taken the gods, Jacob said that the person responsible would die. Though Laban never discovered that his younger daughter was the thief, her untimely death, according to the rabbis, was due to Jacob's hasty words. (*Ecclesiastes Rabbah* 10.4[1])

And so it went on. But Jacob had his way of getting back at my father. He began to breed inferior cattle for my father's part of the herd, and superior cattle for his.

When my father caught on to this, his attitude toward Jacob changed.

Jacob saw the handwriting on the wall. He called Rachel and me to the field. "Your father is not pleased with me," he told us. "You know how he has cheated me. God has kept me safe so far. Now he tells me it's time to go back to my own land."

For once Rachel and I agreed on something. Our father, Laban, had exploited us as well. The money he saved through Jacob's labor should have gone to us and to our children, but our father had used it all for himself. "If your god tells you to go," we said, "then go."

(Martha Whitmore Hickman)

Dinah

After being brutally raped by Shechem, Dinah has no voice in her brothers' plan for revenge.

The Story

Dinah, the daughter whom Leah had borne to Jacob, went out to visit women of the district, and Shechem, son of Hamor the Hivite, the local prince, saw her. He took her, lay with her, and violated her. But Shechem was deeply attached to Jacob's daughter Dinah; he loved the girl and sought to win her affection. Shechem said to Hamor his father, 'You must get me this girl as my wife.' When Jacob learnt that his daughter Dinah had been dishonoured, his sons were with the herds in the open country, so he held his peace until they came home. Meanwhile Shechem's father Hamor came out to Jacob to talk the matter over with him. When they heard the news Jacob's sons came home from the country; they were distressed and very angry, because in lying with Jacob's daughter Shechem had done what the Israelites hold to be an intolerable outrage. Hamor appealed to them: 'My son Shechem is in love with this girl; I beg you to let him have her as his wife. Let us ally ourselves in marriage; you give us your daughters, and you take ours. If you settle among us, the country is open before you; make your home in it, move about freely, and acquire land of your own.' Shechem said to the girl's father and brothers, 'I am eager to win your favour and I shall give whatever you ask. Fix the bride-price and the gift as high as you like, and I shall give whatever you ask; only, give me the girl in marriage.'

Jacob's sons replied to Shechem and his father Hamor deceitfully, because Shechem had violated their sister Dinah: 'We cannot do this,' they said; 'we cannot give our sister to a man who is uncircumcised, for we look on that as a disgrace. Only on one condition can we give our consent: if you follow our example and have every male among you circumcised, we shall give you our daughters and take yours for ourselves. We will then live among you, and become one people with you. But if you refuse to listen to us and be circumcised, we shall take the girl and go.' Their proposal appeared satisfactory to Hamor and his son Shechem; and the young man, who was held in respect above anyone in his father's house, did not hesitate to do what they had said, because his heart had been captured by Jacob's daughter.

Hamor and Shechem went to the gate of their town and addressed their fellow-townsmen: 'These men are friendly towards us,' they said, 'let them live

49

in our country and move freely in it. The land has room enough for them. Let us marry their daughters and give them ours. But on this condition only will these men agree to live with us as one people: every male among us must be circumcised as they are. Their herds, their livestock, and all their chattels will then be ours. We need only agree to their condition, and then they are free to live with us.' All the able-bodied men agreed with Hamor and his son Shechem, and every able-bodied male among them was circumcised. Then two days later, while they were still in pain, two of Jacob's sons, Simeon and Levi, full brothers to Dinah, after arming themselves with sword, boldly entered the town and killed every male. They cut down Hamor and his son Shechem and took Dinah from Shechem's house and went off. Jacob's other sons came in over the dead bodies and plundered the town which had brought dishonour on their sister. They seized flocks, cattle, donkeys, whatever was inside the town and outside in the open country; they carried off all the wealth, the women, and the children, and looted everything in the houses.

Jacob said to Simeon and Levi, 'You have brought trouble on me; you have brought my name into bad odour among the people of the country, the Canaanites and the Perizzites. My numbers are few; if they combine against me and attack, I shall be destroyed, I and my household with me.' They answered, 'Is our sister to be treated as a common whore?'

Comments on the Story

Dinah's life is marred by tragedy. It is sad, but appropriate, that she has no voice in this narrative. From the beginning to the end, she is a victim acted upon by Shechem, Hamor, Jacob, Simeon, Levi, and the rest of her brothers.

Note the context of this account. Jacob and his family have arrived in Canaan, having escaped Laban's treachery in Paddan-aram. Yet even in Canaan they face threats from other peoples. In the previous chapter Jacob feared his encounter with Esau, although the tension was resolved. Seemingly at peace, Jacob settles near Shechem and conducts a legal transaction with the owners to establish his people's legitimacy.

Jacob's peace in the region, however, is threatened by a family dispute that starts when Dinah innocently takes a walk, visiting the women of the area. She is not described as doing anything that would provoke an attack; no one can claim she is a blameworthy victim. When Shechem, the son of Hamor, the local prince of the land, sees her, he attacks. The Hebrew of verse 2 stresses his violence. Literally translated, it reads, "He took her, lay her, and mishandled her." As quickly as he attacked her, however, he had a change of heart. Although we never see Dinah's perspective, Shechem's love for Dinah is presented as being sincere because it is given from the omniscient narrator's perspective. Only after Shechem's feelings are explained does the narrator turn again to dialogue.

Jacob hears of the rape of his daughter before he is approached by Hamor and Shechem; apparently it has become public knowledge. In contrast to his great emotional torment, which occurs later when his sons Joseph and Benjamin are missing, Jacob's emotional distance from Dinah is striking. He hesitates before he speaks, waiting for his sons to return from the fields. His reticence to speak about the attack sets the stage for his sons' quest for revenge. In contrast to Jacob's silence and absence of emotional reaction, the narrator tells the reader that the sons are outraged as soon as they hear of it. Yet they too wait before they speak.

The negotiations begin with the continuation of this conspiracy of silence; no one specifies what has happened to Dinah. Hamor speaks first. Making no reference to the rape, he refers first to Shechem's love for Dinah and desire for marriage, thereby using the opportunity to attempt to develop closer ties between his people and the Israelites. He speaks of marriages between the two peoples, property purchases, and freedom of movement in their territory. Shechem speaks second and addresses Jacob and Dinah's brothers. He appears sincere in his desire to atone for his crime by offering to pay any bride-price that they would determine. Nonetheless, as do all the male characters in this scene, he neither speaks about the rape nor acknowledges his responsibility. Although it is shocking to modern sensibilities, the Bible specifies that if a man lies with (or rapes!) an unmarried woman, he is to marry her and cannot divorce her. Otherwise, she would be ineligible for marriage with any other man.

Jacob continues his passivity. The brothers set the terms, but do so duplicitously. Their demand is that all Hivite men be circumcised. Given that circumcision is a sign of the covenant, in effect they are asking the Hivites to become part of the Israelite people and to follow their God. Indeed, sociological analysis of the Hebrew Bible suggests that indigenous Canaanites did join the Israelite movement. But here the insincerity of the brothers is demeaning to the sign of the covenant. They use the tactic only to weaken the Hivites before their planned attack.

When Hamor and Shechem appeal to their townsmen to be circumcised, they stress the economic advantages that their people would gain by associating with the Israelites. On the one hand, this explanation makes them appear opportunistic, and the lack of any mention of Shechem's love for Dinah makes his devotion to her appear insincere. On the other hand, Hamor's and Shechem's speeches may be clever tactics to make the citizenry accept what would surely be an unpopular decision. They may simply be acting as clever politicians; their people agree to the terms.

The Hivites' acquiescence and agreement to circumcision, however, leads not to peace but rather allows Jacob's sons to have an advantage while staging the attack. Simeon and Levi, two of Leah's full brothers, direct the killing of all the Hivites as an act of revenge. Hamor and Shechem are specified among the deceased. All the other brothers participate in the violence by plundering the town. In this description of the killing and looting, two items are arresting.

First, we learn that Dinah has remained in Shechem's house, presumably as his wife. She is now violated a second time: Her brothers have murdered her husband and violently taken her away from her new home. As the powerless victim, it is not surprising that she continues to have no voice in this story. Second, Dinah is not the only defenseless person who is abused. The other brothers not only plunder goods and steal animals, but they also victimize the women and children. We do not hear what happened to these victims, but the description powerfully contributes to the theme of the anarchy of revenge.

Jacob breaks his long silence at the end of this tragic tale and realizes the long-term political consequences of his brash sons' actions. He laments that other Canaanites can attack him just as his sons raided the Hivites. He continues to ignore his daughter Dinah, however; no mention is made of her. When the sons defend themselves, they do refer to Dinah's violation, but their defense is challenged by their duplicity, their wanton disregard for the sign of the covenant, their lack of direct communication or concern for Dinah, and their destruction of innocent people.

The narrator has tried to present the complexities and nuances in this difficult account. The violence to Dinah was rightfully troubling to her brothers, and their attack was motivated by their outrage. Although the brothers were deceitful, the Hivites were duplicitous as well by never acknowledging the rape of Dinah and by appearing to be motivated by profit when they discussed the intended results of the circumcision with their fellow citizens. Nonetheless, the wanton destruction of life has Jacob genuinely frightened for his family's settlement in the region, and the promise of land and people again appears threatened. Indeed, in the subsequent chapter, God must instill fear into the local Canaanite population in order that the Israelites may travel without being attacked.

The disregard for Dinah is apparent in this entire narrative. Shechem, Hamor, Jacob, and her brothers all use her for their own ends. Her powerlessness appeals to our sympathies, not only for her own sake, but because of the ensuing violence and desire for revenge that result when any people is objectified.

Retelling the Story

She hated it when her brothers talked about her in her presence, because they always treated her as if she were in a coma, or worse, a piece of dead wood. They never talked to her, asked her feelings, her opinion. They talked about her as if she were one of their donkeys or camels, and she knew that

52

though they spoke of their love for her as their sister, she was considered little more than livestock.

> The rabbis portray Dinah's brothers as having little sympathy or even regard for their sister's feelings. If anything, they—and sometimes the rabbis—blamed Dinah for having gone out of her father's house in the first place. Her brothers' callousness is demonstrated by their response to their sister's violation. When they heard that Shechem had raped Dinah, they were enraged and said, "How dare this heathen treat us like some object he can use at will!" They are so worried about their own honor that they never acknowledge that it was their sister who had been ill used. (*Genesis Rabbah* 80.2)

Such was the situation for a woman of the Middle East. Each morning men thanked God they had not been born female. Here sons were called "ben," or "son of," followed by their father's name, though it was their mothers who bled and screamed, nursed and wept over them. Here fathers' names were changed when a son arrived and were called "abu," or "father of," their eldest son. Daughters were considered a liability.

For all the differences among the many tribes that fought and killed each other over these hillsides and grazing lands, they were bound together by at least two firmly held convictions. These were a mutual distrust for anyone who was different and the idea that women were the property of men.

Dinah's current predicament was the perfect example. Shechem had raped her; there was no other word for it. It was brutal and humiliating. She had done nothing to provoke this young stranger's attention. Even so, throughout the attack he acted as if she had been the instigator. "You wanted it," he kept repeating. All she really wanted was for this living nightmare to be over. Even after the initial physical pain began to subside, waves of nausea swept over her, and what she wished more than anything in the world was that he had killed her instead.

> The brothers who take revenge on Shechem and his people are not viewed as heroes by the sages. They make it clear that while Simeon and Levi are full brothers to Dinah, they are only half-brothers to Joseph. These two who took such violent revenge for the violation of "their honor" in the rape of their sister also speak evil against Joseph. Though the specific brothers go unnamed in Genesis, the sages contend that Simeon and Levi argue for taking Joseph's life, while Judah and Reuben seek ways to save their brother. (*Genesis Rabbah* 98.5)

Now her brothers were shouting in angry voices about how *their* honor had been violated, and their eyes burned with revenge for what had happened to *them*. "Stop it!" she heard her own voice repeating more loudly each time she said it. But her brothers gave no indication that they heard her. Were her screams on the inside only, so that her pain was unheard by any human ear other than her own? Did God hear her, or was her God just a larger version of her brothers, railing against offenses, against some divine code of honor while all the time ignoring her hurt?

Now the voices around her were whispers, as if their shouts for revenge had transformed to plotting it. She heard the words "foreskins," "the sign of Abraham," and "marriage." Surely they did not intend to give her in marriage to her rapist, even if he did agree to be circumcised! Not even her brothers could be that insensitive to her plight. Would they sacrifice their sister when Abraham had not sacrificed his son? She wept and prayed for a lamb in the thicket, for some way out of such an unimaginable fate. Could the same God the men invoked in their battles against their enemies also be called to the side of a woman violated by her enemy, ignored by her family, and traded like a donkey?

Some say that Dinah later married Job and counseled her husband to "curse God and die" in response to his unmerited suffering. Some rabbis suggest that Job sinned in accusing his wife of lacking piety and in his mild rebuke, "If we accept good from God shall we not accept evil?" The sages defend the righteousness of Dinah in spite of her radical suggestion for escaping suffering. Perhaps they intuited that this woman had already experienced more than her share of unmerited suffering. (*Genesis Rabbah* 19.12)

Is there no God, her inner voice pleaded, *beyond my brothers' imagining; a God who knows the hurts of the abused and brokenhearted? Is there no God with the heart of a mother to hear her children and weep for their injuries? Is there no God?* (Michael E. Williams)

Tamar

After the death of her husband, Tamar takes drastic measures to get her father-in-law to abide by the law of levirate marriage and conceive a son with her.

The Story

About that time Judah parted from his brothers, and heading south he pitched his tent in company with an Adullamite named Hirah. There he saw Bathshua the daughter of a Canaanite and married her. He lay with her, and she conceived and bore a son, whom she called Er. She conceived again and bore a son, whom she called Onan. Once more she conceived and bore a son whom she called Shelah, and she was at Kezib when she bore him. Judah found a wife for his eldest son Er; her name was Tamar. But Judah's eldest son Er was wicked in the LORD's sight, and the LORD took away his life. Then Judah told Onan to sleep with his brother's wife, to do his duty as the husband's brother and raise up offspring for his brother. But Onan knew that the offspring would not count as his; so whenever he lay with his brother's wife, he spilled his seed on the ground so as not to raise up offspring for his brother. What he did was wicked in the LORD's sight, and the LORD took away his life also. Judah said to his daughter-in-law Tamar, 'Remain as a widow in your father's house until my son Shelah grows up'; for he was afraid that Shelah too might die like his brothers. So

Tamar went and stayed in her father's house.

Time passed, and Judah's wife Bathshua died. When he had finished mourning, he and his friend Hirah the Adullamite went up to Timnath at sheep-shearing. When Tamar was told that he father-in-law was on his way to shear his sheep at Timnath, she took off her widow's clothes, covered her face with a veil, and then sat where the road forks on the way to Timnath. She did this because she saw that although Shelah was now grown up she had not been given to him as a wife. When Judah saw her he thought she was a prostitute, for she had veiled her face. He turned to her where she sat by the roadside and said, 'Let me lie with you,' not realizing she was his daughter-in-law. She said, 'What will you give to lie with me?'

He answered, 'I shall send you a young goat from my flock.' She said, 'I agree if you will give me a pledge until you send it.' He asked what pledge he should give her, and she replied, 'Your seal and its cord, and the staff which you are holding.' He handed them over to her and lay with her, and she became pregnant. She then rose and went home, where she took off her veil and put on her widow's clothes again.

Judah sent the goat by his friend the Adullamite in order to recover the pledge from the woman, but he could not find her. When he enquired of the people of that place, 'Where is that temple-prostitute, the one who was sitting where the road forks?' they answered, 'There has been no temple-prostitute here.' So he went back to Judah and reported that he had failed to find her and that the men of the place had said there was no such prostitute there. Judah said, 'Let her keep the pledge, or we shall be a laughing-stock. After all, I did send the kid, even though you could not find her.'

About three months later Judah was told that his daughter-in-law Tamar had played the prostitute and got herself pregnant. 'Bring her out,' ordered Judah, 'so that she may be burnt.' But as she was being brought out, she sent word to her father-in-law. 'The father of my child is the man to whom these things belong,' she said. 'See if you recognize whose they are, this seal, the pattern of the cord, and the staff.' Judah identified them and said, 'She is more in the right than I am, because I did not give her to my son Shelah.' He did not have intercourse with her again.

When her time was come, she was found to have twins in her womb, and while she was in labour one of them put out a hand. The midwife took a scarlet thread and fastened it round the wrist, saying, 'This one appeared first.' No sooner had he drawn back his hand, than his brother came out and the midwife said, 'What! You have broken out first!' So he was named Perez. Soon afterwards his brother was born with the scarlet thread on his wrist, and he was named Zerah.

Comments on the Story

The context of the narrative of Tamar is the Joseph cycle—the account of the Israelites' descent into Egypt because of Jacob's sons' betrayal of their father's favorite son, Joseph. In Genesis 38, the narrator seems to digress to tell the story of another son of Jacob, Judah, and his daughter-in-law Tamar. The account is told for its own sake: the quest for justice by the righteous Tamar. But in addition, by the narrator's placement of this story within the Joseph cycle, the account comments on the necessity for Judah's recognition of justice, thus preparing the reader for his future role within the broader narrative. Earlier, Judah first instigated the sale of his brother into slavery, but after this text, we find it is also Judah who offers his own life for the safety of his brother Benjamin.

The account begins with descriptions of Judah's activity, which prompt the reader to question his judgment. He parts with his brothers, lives among Canaanites, and marries a Canaanite woman, Bathshua (literally, "the daughter of Sua"). The names of their sons—Er, Onan, and Shelah—are chosen by Bathshua, indicative of their Canaanite inheritance and the clash of values between Canaanites and Israelites. Er, who is deemed wicked by God, who takes his life, means "exposed." Onan, who despicably withholds his progeny from Tamar, ironically means "vigorous," and Shelah, who is withheld from Tamar by Judah and thus is a silent character, means "quiet."

Who is this Tamar who is associated with Judah and his sons? We are not told her origins—only that Judah obtained her as his first son's wife. In context, because Judah is living in Canaanite land, it is likely that she is meant to be thought of as Canaanite. If so, she forms a thorough contrast to her husband, Er, and brother-in-law Onan. If she is meant to be considered an Israelite, she forms an excellent contrast in character to her father-in-law, Judah.

Judah's request to have Onan complete sexual relations with Tamar may at first appear strange to the modern reader, but this practice, the levirate obligation of marriage, was a recorded law among the Israelites. If a man died without leaving any offspring, his brother or next of kin was obligated to provide a child in the name of the brother. The child was considered the dead relative's legal offspring, and the progenitor of the offspring had no rights concerning this child and his inheritance. Sometimes the man would also marry (and provide) for the woman, but it is not clear whether this was a requirement of the law. Onan's refusal to provide Tamar with a child is reprehensible. He does not refuse to lie with her; rather, he uses her sexually, while preventing her from becoming pregnant by climaxing outside of her. Tamar suffers first from her widowhood and second by Onan's treachery. We must remember that being a childless widow was a particular hardship in Israel because in most cases women could not inherit an estate or provide for themselves. The frequent references in the Bible to the community's responsibility to widows and orphans indicate that these groups were in need of societal support.

Judah considers neither Tamar's feelings nor his sons' sins. Rather, he assumes that Tamar is responsible for Er's and Onan's deaths, blaming the victim simply because she was associated with them. Like Onan, he denies his responsibility and deceives her. Judah demands that Tamar live in her own father's house while waiting until his third son, Shelah, grows up and can fulfill the levirate obligation. The expected custom, however, was for the widow to stay in the father-in-law's house. Judah is obviously lying to her, as the narrator indicates, and has no intention of ever allowing Shelah to be near her.

In the next scene, circumstances have changed, allowing Tamar, the woman of lesser power and authority, to demand justice from Judah. Tamar cannot do so forthrightly, however, but must use deception and cleverness. The stage is set: Judah has become a widower and travels to Tamar's vicinity for sheepshearing. He has not communicated with her directly for some time; she hears of his visit through others. Recognizing that Shelah has grown up and has been denied to her, she attempts to make contact with Judah. She dresses as a prostitute, but the narrator, by stating her reason, is careful not to condemn her. In contrast to the years of Tamar's isolation, Judah, who has just completed his mourning period, appears desirous for sex. Tamar is not presented as a temptress, but her mere presence, dressed as a prostitute, prompts Judah to approach her and request intercourse. Taking advantage of his initiative, Tamar finds an unexpected way to become pregnant through her husband's line by using Judah himself. For the first time in the narrative, Tamar speaks. Her discourse with Judah is intended to give her the means to prove the paternity of the child. She suggests what the pledge for Judah's payment should be: his signet, cord, and staff, specifically marked items indicating ownership. Tamar immediately becomes pregnant. In order to stress that her guise of prostitution was strictly utilitarian, the narrator confirms that she quickly puts on her widow's clothing again.

Judah's casual attitude toward the incident is reflected by the means he employs to bring the payment of the goat and to retrieve his items of pledge; he uses his friend Hirah the Adullamite. It is appropriate, then, that Judah has no hope of being reunited with his things if he does not take the trouble to find the woman himself. Indeed, while looking for Tamar, Hirah uses the wrong word to describe her. In Hebrew there are two words for prostitutes: *qedeshah,* or cultic prostitute, and *zonah,* or common prostitute. Tamar had appeared as a common prostitute, whereas Hirah presumes Judah associated with a cultic prostitute, a characteristic of Canaanite worship practice, and frequently condemned by Israelite authorities. Thus when Hirah inquires about the whereabouts of the cultic prostitute, the townspeople respond that no such person has been there. Judah has no choice but to allow Tamar to keep the identifying pledge.

When Judah hears that Tamar is pregnant, he takes the authority upon himself to act as judge and condemns her with a horrifying punishment: death by burning. The dignity with which Tamar responds reveals her equanimity in spite of her powerlessness. Instead of directly accusing the guilty party, she allows Judah to discover for himself that he is the father and that he has done her a terrible injustice. She says, "The father of my child is the man to whom these things belong," (v. 25), allowing Judah to entertain the possibility that he can condemn another person—there is evidence to be used against the responsible man! Only after revealing the existence of the evidence does she tell him to note the specific items. When he does so, Judah finally acknowledges that he is responsible for Tamar's plight because he was wrong in not giving Shelah to her. Sadly, the injustice is not completely rectified, because we do not read of Judah giving Shelah to Tamar or providing for her. Is it simply the case that because she is pregnant she is now provided for? Perhaps, but the question is not fully resolved.

The injustice of Judah's withholding of children to Tamar is especially emphasized by the end of this narrative. Tamar's pregnancy results in twins, one of whom has particular importance in Israel's history. Perez's significance is first indicated by his unexpected birth order as the firstborn son. Perez is the ancestor of King David, the recipient of an eternal covenant with God. Thus David can trace his ancestry back to the courageous Tamar who used her sagacity to be certain that her right to have children was not denied by unjust men.

Retelling the Story

Well, what would you think, if one day you were standing in the line at the grocery store and you picked up a copy of *The National Intruder,* only to see your own face staring back at you? The first thing I did was to look around to see if anybody else in the store had noticed that I was the one who was plastered all over the cover in a picture that was so grainy it looked as if it had been taken through the bottom of a fruit jar. I just slipped the paper back into its rack, back page facing out, and left my basket sitting right there in line. Of course, I made the kind of exasperated noise you make when you've forgotten something and have to run to aisle six to get it and won't be gone but a second. Then I slipped through the produce section and out the door.

You may have read about my situation by now, but just in case you haven't, here it is. I'm getting ready to have my mother-in-law's baby by my father-in-law. Now, get your mind out of the gutter. It's not what you're thinking. The papers make it sound trashy, but believe me it's not. Actually, it's kind of a long story.

Back when Ernie married me, he knew I wanted a family, but I'll tell you the truth, he seemed interested in everything else but having children. First, he talked me into going on the pill, just until we could get ahead enough to afford a baby—or that's what he said. But by the time I wised up and decided that my husband was going to spend all his time with his buddies at some beer joint and spend all our money on "tall cold ones" and the poker machines, it was too late. He just stopped taking any interest in me, and after a while he just quit coming home. And when he did find his way to the house, he was too drunk to "do his duty," if you know what I mean.

In the third month of her pregnancy it became clear to the world that Tamar would bear a child, though her husband was dead and her brother-in-law Onan had refused to "do his duty." But Tamar was clearly no wilting flower in the face of adversity or accusations. When people accused her of becoming pregnant through prostitution, she would slap her growing stomach and say, "I carry within me kings and redeemers." (*Genesis Rabbah* 85.10)

Then one night the police came to the door and told me that Ernie had been killed in a wreck, driving under the influence as they put it, which they didn't even have to say, since I would have guessed that anyway. I just cried my heart out at the funeral, although I wasn't crying for Ernie so much as I was for myself. After all, how do you miss somebody who isn't ever there anyway? I think his family knew that I was crying for the babies I would never have. That may be why Ernie's brother Hershel came over a few nights later and said what he did to me. Honestly, I don't think the baby was the part that he had in mind, if you know what I mean. I told him, "Hershel, I hope you're drunk and not just crazy. Otherwise I'd shoot you where you stand for even suggesting such a thing." He mumbled something about just wanting to help out as he tripped going down the front steps.

Truth is I did want a baby, I just couldn't stand the thought of Hershel getting close enough to touch me, much less us having a baby together. That's when I came up with this other idea. I had seen this woman on "Oprah" who was having a baby for another woman. I think they were sisters or something. *Well,* I thought to myself, *I don't have a sister, but I do have a mother-in-law. She ought to owe me something for taking that jerk of a son off her hands so he could ruin my life instead of hers!*

So I called Nadine on the phone and told her to come over for coffee some Saturday morning soon, because I had something to talk over with her. When she came she didn't seem to warm up to the idea right away. But when I explained that it would be just as easy as pie to get a doctor to take that old fertilized egg out of her and put it in me and that it wouldn't cost her a cent. You see, I took out a life insurance policy on Ernie when we first got married that ought to just about pay for it. And who knows, the health policy down at the plant might even cover part of it. The kicker was when I told her that this way she could get a grandchild by her having all the fun and me doing all the work.

Well, it wasn't three months before she came to me with the good news. One night after Clyde had finished watching a particularly stimulating movie on TV the deal was done, if you know what I mean. The doctor was all lined up, and the switch was made. Now I'm in my eighth month, as big as the side of a house and happy as a hog in mud. I get to have the baby I think God wanted me to have all along, and Nadine gets a grandbaby. It's not that I'm not sorry about Ernie and all, but it will be easier without having two babies to take care of, if you know what I mean.

Now, some people think what I did was trashy; you might even think so. But it doesn't matter to me. I don't care what you or *The National Intruder* thinks. I'm gonna love this baby like it was my very own, and in a way it is, if you know what I mean. *(Michael E. Williams)*

Twin sons were born to Tamar by Judah, Perez and Zerah. Much later these two would be identified as the twins of the zodiac by certain of the sages attempting a specifically Jewish interpretation of the astrologers' art. (*Esther Rabbah* 7.11)

Shiphrah and Puah

Two midwives risk their own lives to save those of the Hebrew children in Pharaoh's slave camps.

The Story

In course of time Joseph and all his brothers and that entire generation died. The Israelites were prolific and increased greatly, becoming so numerous and strong that the land was full of them. When a new king ascended the throne of Egypt, one who did not know about Joseph, he said to his people, 'These Israelites have become too many and too strong for us. We must take steps to ensure that they increase no further; otherwise we shall find that, if war comes, they will side with the enemy, fight against us, and become masters of the country.' So taskmasters were appointed over them to oppress them with forced labour. This is how Pharaoh's store cities, Pithom and Rameses, were built. But the more oppressive the treatment of the Israelites, the more they increased and spread, until the Egyptians came to loathe them. They ground down their Israelite slaves, and made life bitter for them with their harsh demands, setting them to make mortar and bricks and to do all sorts of tasks in the fields. In every kind of labour they made ruthless use of them.

The king of Egypt issued instructions to the Hebrew midwives, of whom one was called Shiphrah, the other Puah.

'When you are attending the Hebrew women in childbirth,' he told them, 'check as the child is delivered: if it is a boy, kill him; if it is a girl, however, let her live.' But the midwives were god-fearing women, and did not heed the king's words; they let the male children live. Pharaoh summoned the midwives and, when he asked them why they had done this and let the male children live, they answered, 'Hebrew women are not like Egyptian women; they go into labour and give birth before the midwife arrives.' God made the midwives prosper, and the people increased in numbers and strength; and because the midwives feared God he gave them families of their own. Pharaoh then issued an order to all the Egyptians that every new-born Hebrew boy was to be thrown into the Nile, but all the girls were to be allowed to live.

A certain man, a descendant of Levi, married a Levite woman. She conceived and bore a son, and when she saw what a fine child he was, she kept him hidden for three months. Unable to conceal him any longer, she got a rush basket for him, made it watertight with pitch and tar, laid him in it, and placed it among the reeds by the bank of the Nile. The child's sister stood some distance away to see what would happen to him.

Pharaoh's daughter came down to bathe in the river, while her ladies-in-waiting walked on the bank. She noticed the basket among the reeds and sent her slave-girl to bring it. When she opened it, there was the baby; it was crying, and she was moved with pity for it. 'This must be one of the Hebrew children,' she said. At this the sister approached Pharaoh's daughter: 'Shall I go and fetch you one of the Hebrew women to act as a wet-nurse for the child?' When Pharaoh's daughter told her to do so, she went and called the baby's mother. Pharaoh's daughter said to her, 'Take the child, nurse him for me, and I shall pay you for it.' She took the child and nursed him at her breast. Then, when he was old enough, she brought him to Pharaoh's daughter, who adopted him and called him Moses, 'because,' she said, 'I drew him out of the water.'

Comments on the Story

The well-known story of the Exodus forms the paradigm for salvation in the Hebrew Scriptures. The Lord who intervenes is the God who saves the community from oppression. The salvation from oppressive governmental and societal systems in Egypt is repeated throughout Israel's history as God delivers the Israelites from the unjust policies of other governments as well.

As this early scene from Exodus opens, times have changed for the Israelites, who once enjoyed favor with the Egyptians. Some scholars locate the historical setting of the account to the reign of Rameses II (1290–1224 B.C.E.) who, like his father Seti I, was wary of foreigners. These pharaohs were unlike their Hyksos predecessors who, perhaps being of Semitic origin themselves, were disposed to favor the Hebrews. Even if these historical allusions have been misidentified, the charge that foreigners are different and to be feared is common. In this xenophobic atmosphere, the Hebrews are oppressed with the burden of Egypt's forced building projects. The use of repetition in verses 11-14, wherein the description of the Egyptians' ruthless oppression is given several times emphasizes the Israelites' plight.

With this dire scene painted, life for the Israelites becomes even more threatened. Pharaoh orders the Hebrew midwives Shiphrah and Puah to kill all the newborn male children (the boys pose more of a threat than the girls because as adults they are more feared by the state). Much of the story of Shiphrah and Puah is lost. It is striking that their names are preserved; usually in such brief accounts the women remain nameless. Their role is brief but crucial to the survival of the Israelite people, who proclaim throughout the Exodus story that their God does not tolerate oppression, and gives them the covenant at Sinai, which endures throughout Israel's history.

From the omniscient narrator's perspective we learn about the strong characters of Shiphrah and Puah; they are "god fearing women" (v. 17). When questioned by Pharaoh, they express no fear. Their statement that the Hebrew women are strong and thus give birth before the midwives arrive is clever. Pharaoh, a man of royalty, would presumably know nothing about birthing practices, so Shiphrah and Puah can use this excuse. At the same time, they compliment Hebrew women by referring to their unusual strength, in contrast to Egyptian women. Pharaoh, who has the power of life and death over slave women, is tricked. Shiphrah and Puah, who have no power and authority of their own, have used their intelligence to protect future generations of Israelites. God rewards them with families; the blessing of children is highly regarded as God's gift throughout the Hebrew Bible.

Although Pharaoh is duped by Shiphrah and Puah, his reign of terror escalates. He counters with a plan that the Hebrew girls will be allowed to live and to be used as he wills, but the more threatening boys are to be thrown into the Nile. Ironically, the river that gives life to otherwise barren Egypt is now to be the place of death for Hebrew boys. But this ominous scene sets the stage for the courageous intervention of other women who save the life of Israel's teacher and law giver in the book of Exodus: Moses. Moses, who guides his people through the Red Sea and receives God's commandments on Mount Sinai is not deified in the Hebrew Bible, but he is regarded as Israel's greatest prophet. The Israelites owe Moses' life to the intervention of his resourceful mother and sister and the sympathetic daughter of Pharaoh, whose names are never mentioned in this particular story.

The account of Moses in the bulrushes parallels that of the Egyptian legend of Sargon—another hero rescued from the Nile. Whatever the legendary qualities of this account, the narrator's purpose in using it is to highlight God's protection of Israel and God's ability to defeat the whims of Pharaoh, who, in Egypt, was considered a god. Indeed, the early chapters of the book of Exodus depict a contest between the God of Israel and the gods of Egypt, represented by Pharaoh.

As chapter 2 begins, we learn of Moses' background: both parents are Levites, thus establishing Moses' priestly lineage. The courage of Moses' mother is immediately identified. She hides him for three months, and when she puts him in a basket in the Nile, she is careful to make it waterproof with two substances. In addition, Moses' sister stands watch. Later texts in Exodus and Numbers identify Moses' mother as Jochebed and sister as Miriam. Some modern scholars, however, suggest that the genealogy identifying Moses' mother comes from tradition and that a girl other than Miriam may have been meant in the original narrative. Nonetheless, these debated issues do not detract from the important roles Moses' mother and sister play in the opening chapters of Exodus as they stand in their final version.

Introducing an element of the unexpected, the narrator shows that the next woman responsible for saving Moses is an Egyptian! Not only is she from

Israel's enemies, but she is Pharaoh's daughter. Unlike her father, who issues the death decree, she sends another woman to get the basket—her slave (a Hebrew?)—and pities the crying baby. At this point, Moses' sister acts with courage. She approaches Pharaoh's daughter and makes a bold request, asking if she can obtain a Hebrew nurse for the baby. Pharaoh's daughter agrees, and thus Moses' own mother is obtained to nurse him. Although Pharaoh's daughter later names and adopts Moses, the narrator introduces the possibility that Moses learns about his own traditions from his mother, who cared for him. Indeed, the scene that follows shows that Moses' feelings are for his fellow Hebrews, with whom he clearly identifies.

Shiphrah, Puah, Moses' mother and sister, and Pharaoh's daughter feature prominently in the opening section of the book of Exodus. The midwives' actions show that even slaves can foil the most cruel designs of Pharaoh. Moses' mother and sister show that courage and cunning can lead to safety. The kindness of Pharaoh's daughter contrasts with her father's cruelty, helping to balance the image of Egyptians in the book. The actions of these women are extraordinary and help to prepare the reader for the miracles that occur throughout the book of Exodus for this oppressed people.

Retelling the Story

Shiphrah awoke in the darkness and quiet of early morning. The only sound breaking through the silence was her name. Someone was calling her. It was a child's voice. Was this her recurring dream a vision of the children to whom she would never give birth? The dream came more frequently as she had grown older. As Rachel had wept for her children and grandchildren, Shiphrah's eyes flooded for those she would never see. She had assisted so many other women into the joy and pain of motherhood, only to be denied both herself. All she knew was loss and emptiness in her own womb.

The voice was no dream, though. It pierced her door and the darkness of her room. As the voice pulled her toward wakefulness, she began to recognize that this was the voice of some older sister or brother summoning her to come to God's (and some mother's) aid in bringing a child into the world.

According to the rabbis, midwives had a special place of trust among the people. They were one of only three groups of people whose word was taken at face value without question or corroborating testimony. (*Genesis Rabbah* 85.13)

"Hurry!" the voice cried out. "There's not much time," it insisted. She rose and followed the child through the mud streets of the Hebrew slave quarters. When she arrived, Shiphrah discovered the urgency in the child's pleas had not been exaggerated. The mother was squatting, and the baby's head had already emerged. The midwife had arrived just in time to "catch" the baby, clean it up, and place it on its exhausted mother's breast. The new, high-pitched voice could be heard throughout the house, and likely in the houses of neighbors as well.

When the child was not screaming its objection to its new, cold surroundings, its tiny mouth would purse, seeking nourishment. As Shiphrah placed the newborn into its mother's arms, she thought of how death attached itself to each of us like a shadow. The brighter our life at any moment, the deeper death's presence there next to us. Shiphrah walked back to her room just as light crept down the soft pathways between slave dwellings. The child had been male, she thought. She was under Pharaoh's orders to kill all the boy babies of the Hebrew slaves. She had refused to carry out his commands, though she knew the penalty could cost her own life.

She had been terribly frightened when she and Puah had been directed to appear before Pharaoh. "I am ruler of all that is," he boasted, "and I order you to kill all the newborn Hebrew boys. Smother the life out of them, then tell the mother they were born dead. That's simple enough, isn't it?" Even as the hateful edict was given, Shiphrah was distracted.

As soon as she and Puah had entered the room, Shiphrah had been overwhelmed by an odor she recognized

> Some of the sages identify the two midwives as Jochebed and Miriam, the mother and sister of Moses. They say that Miriam, though only five years old at the time, would help her mother with the delivery and entertain the baby by blowing bubbles while Jochebed looked after the new mother. (*Exodus Rabbah* 1.13)

but could not quite name. At first she thought it was a spice or perfume brought from some far-off land to sweeten Pharaoh's surroundings. As soon as the words of death emerged from Pharaoh's mouth, she knew what it was. Among all the other exotic aromas that filled the courtroom was the undeniable smell of fear.

She had failed to recognize it because she was used to smelling fear in the dark slave quarters where some first-time mother was about to give birth. Suddenly she realized that this man who claimed to rule all that is was scared to death of his own Hebrew slaves.

The midwives left Pharaoh's presence in silence. His assumption that he was in charge was so all pervasive that he didn't even wait for their consent to his murderous plan. He simply assumed that because he said it, it would be done. After all, he thought, he was in control of everything in his realm and that each of his orders would be carried out without question.

As they began to recover from Pharaoh's horrifying directive, Shiphrah and Puah began to talk. How could they possibly ever consider doing what he commanded? They knew that they did not control the process of birth any more than they could control the conception of life. God brought new lives to birth while midwives, and even the mother, only assisted in the process. Both midwives agreed that they could no more end the life of a newborn than they could give it life in the first place.

What would they tell Pharaoh then? One who assumes he controls everything could not begin to comprehend that he did not control what God was bringing to birth in the Hebrew slave camps. Puah recalled a recent experience when she had arrived late for a birth. The child was already screaming for its mother's touch and warmth by the time Puah arrived. Shiphrah had many such stories, too.

They would simply tell Pharaoh the truth. The Hebrew women were so strong that the children are born before we arrive. Perhaps he could understand that.

Shiphrah washed her hands and face. It was too far into the morning to return to bed. God had brought the child, as God had brought the day. She waited to see what else God would bring out of the muddy streets of the slave quarters. *(Michael E. Williams)*

The names of the two midwives, Shiphrah and Puah, are symbolic of the function each serves in the story. Some say that Shiphrah helped make the newborn beautiful to look at, or that she helped Israel to multiply, or that her acts were pleasing to God, because her name is similar to Hebrew words for those activities. Puah is said to have revived infants others said were dead, and that she spoke in such a forthright and angry manner when Pharaoh asked her to kill Hebrew babies that he wanted to have her killed, since her name sounds like similar terms in Hebrew. (*Exodus Rabbah* 1.13)

EXODUS 15:1-21

Miriam

After the Israelites pass to safety through the sea, Miriam and Moses lead in a song of victory.

The Story

Then Moses and the Israelites sang
   this song to the LORD:
"I shall sing to the LORD, for he has
   risen up in triumph;
horse and rider he has hurled into
   the sea.
The LORD is my refuge and my
   defence;
he has shown himself my deliverer.
He is my God, and I shall glorify
   him;
my father's God, and I shall exalt
   him.
The LORD is a warrior; the LORD is
   his name.
Pharaoh's chariots and his army
he has cast into the sea;
the flower of his officers
are engulfed in the Red Sea.
The watery abyss has covered them;
they sank to the depths like a stone.
Your right hand, LORD, is majestic in
   strength;
your right hand, LORD, shattered the
   enemy.
In the fullness of your triumph
you overthrew those who opposed
   you:
   you let loose your fury;
it consumed them like stubble.
At the blast of your anger the sea
   piled up;

the water stood up like a bank;
out at sea the great deep congealed.
'The enemy boasted, "I shall pursue,
   I shall overtake;
I shall divide the spoil,
I shall glut my appetite on them;
I shall draw my sword,
I shall rid myself of them."
You blew with your blast; the sea
   covered them;
they sank like lead in the swelling
   waves.
'LORD, who is like you among the
   gods?
Who is like you, majestic in holiness,
worthy of awe and praise, worker of
   wonders?
You stretched out your right hand;
the earth engulfed them.
'In your constant love you led the
   people
whom you had redeemed:
you guided them by your strength
to your holy dwelling-place.
Nations heard and trembled;
anguish seized the dwellers in
   Philistia.
The chieftains of Edom were then
   dismayed.
trembling seized the leaders of Moab,
the inhabitants of Canaan were all
   panic-stricken;

67

terror and dread fell upon them:
through the might of your arm
they stayed stone-still
while your people passed, LORD,
while the people whom you made
   your own passed by.
You will bring them in and plant
   them
in the mount that is your possession,
the dwelling-place, LORD, of your
   own making,
the sanctuary, LORD, which your
   own hands established.
The LORD will reign for ever and for
   ever.'

When Pharaoh's horse, both chariots
and cavalry, went into the sea, the
LORD brought back the waters over
them; but Israel had passed through the
sea on dry ground. The prophetess Miriam, Aaron's sister, took up her tam-
bourine, and all the women followed
her, dancing to the sound of tambourines; and Miriam sang them this
refrain:
   'Sing to the LORD, for he has risen
     up in triumph:
   horse and rider he has hurled into
     the sea.'

Comments on the Story

It is likely that poetic texts usually had an independent existence before they were incorporated into the prose sections of the Hebrew Scriptures. Exodus 15:1a and 15:19-21 form distinct introductions to the Song of Sea. The first identifies the singers as Moses and the Israelites (men or men and women); the second identifies the singers as Miriam and all the women. Perhaps the redactor of the final edition of Exodus intended the reader to understand that the song was recited twice, first by Moses and all the men, and then by Miriam and all the women. Other scholars debate which superscription is older and more original. Because it is easier to imagine a later author adding Moses' name to this song, some argue that Miriam's association was earlier. The poem is often called the Song of Miriam.

Miriam is identified as Aaron's sister, with no expressed link to Moses. There may have been a time when other traditions circulated about her that no longer remain, because as Moses became more important in the history of Israel, she and Aaron received less recognition. What is known about Miriam here? Identified as a prophet, she would have been an honored member of the community, considered God's spokesperson. Although some prophets were despised, there are no indications of rejection here (however, political problems concerning Miriam's leadership occur later). In addition, the prophet Micah identifies Miriam as an important leader in the days of the Exodus and wilderness wanderings. The book of Micah states

> "I brought you up from the land of Egypt,
>   and redeemed you from the house of slavery;
> and I sent before you Moses,
>   Aaron, and Miriam." (Mic. 6:4)

68

Was Miriam identified as Moses and Aaron's sister? The evidence is uncertain. Two genealogical texts do so: Numbers 26:59 and 1 Chronicles 6:3. The genealogy in Exodus 6:20, however, is silent about Miriam, listing only Moses and Aaron as the children of Amran and Jochebed. In the text considered here, Miriam's identity as Aaron's sister allows her priestly lineage to be emphasized (although women, of course, could not be priests). She is a musician and choral leader, and all the women follow her in singing this song.

Although these brief reports will not allow us to say much about Miriam, there is enough evidence to show that she was a prophet and a leader in the days of the Exodus and the wilderness wanderings. Her voice was heard; the women follow her in prayer, and the prophet Micah credits her role as a leader. Other stories were told about her but were suppressed after her conflict with Moses, which will be discussed in the next section.

Let us turn now to the content of the poem associated with Miriam, highlighting key phrases. In verse 1, the LORD as warrior has destroyed the soldiers and the implements of war, Pharaoh's horses. The LORD has been successful in verse 2 in the ongoing contest with Pharaoh. This God, the warrior against oppression, is the same God of the ancestors (my father's God) who formed the covenant of land, descendants, and blessing. To call the LORD "a warrior," as in verses 3-4, sometimes seems offensive to modern audiences, but the reference need not be, because the context makes clear that God fights oppression and injustice. Verses 5-8 tell us that water and the deep are "weapons" that God uses, along with the metaphor of God's "right arm" against the enemy. Water, at first the enemy of the Israelites because it caged them in around Pharaoh's troops, is now used by the LORD as a weapon and it obeys God's commands. In verses 9-10 the theme of reversal continues. The enemy believes it can overtake the Israelites because they are blocked by the sea. Instead, a simple blast from God forces the sea to drown the enemy. The Exodus began as a contest between the God of Israel and the gods of the Egyptians, represented by Pharaoh. It is now clear in verses 11-12 who the superior God is—the one who is victorious in battle over oppression! Verses 13-18 proclaim that God's deliverance from oppression will continue in Israel's history. The poem recites God's upcoming majestic deeds for the people. They will be brought to Canaan, where other nations threaten them with similar oppressive practices. But again God will deliver them from the unjust Canaanite kings. Hence, panic falls on such leaders as the chiefs of Edom and Moab. The mountain to which the LORD will lead them, verse 17, is not identified. Perhaps the author meant Mount Zaphon, a sacred place in Canaan. A later reader could assume the text refers to Mount Zion, the place where Israel turned its hope that the Torah would go forth to all nations.

Retelling the Story

Shortly before dawn the people of the Hebrews—their shoulders hunched against the wind and blowing spray, their babies held close in the wrapped cloaks of their mothers, the animals following with bleats of protest—cross over the Reed Sea. Line by line, they come, heads down, looking only at the bent figures in the line ahead of them. The wind howls from the east, drives back the sea from the wide carpet of wet sand on which they walk.

In the damp cold, as each line reaches the other side, they turn to stretch helping hands to those behind them. Then they stand, awestruck, watching the rising wall of water on each side of the traverse, murmuring their relief and gratitude against the continuing drone of the wind.

At last they have all come over. They clutch one another for warmth. They exult, "The Lord has brought us through the sea!"

But wait! Looking back the way they have come they see on the opposite shore the chariots and horsemen of Pharaoh approaching the shore, thundering toward the same strip of dry land on which they have crossed over. "No!" they cry, their hopes of safety dashed like waves smashing on rock.

The rabbis suggest that there is a reason why the feminine form of the Hebrew word for "song" is used here. They say that the history of Israel is like a woman who has given birth to many children. Each time there is the stress of pregnancy and the struggle and pain of birth, but each time that difficult process leads to something wonderful: the birth of a child. Just so, each episode of struggle and pain for Israel leads to something better than they ever imagined. That is why they celebrate by singing and why the form of the word is feminine. (*Exodus Rabbah* 23.11)

Miriam, standing in a cluster of wet and bewildered people, watches her brother. What will he do now? In a flash of memory she sees him, all those years, a tiny infant in a basket, adrift to the reedy edge of another body of water, the Nile.

She was there, too, a child herself. Their mother had left her there to watch. No one would suspect a child of defying Pharaoh's order. In the basket her brother slept. He was her baby, her doll, her toy. She would have given her life for him. And then the princess came and took him in her arms, and he was safe. Until that day, years later, when he could bear the abuse of his people no longer and killed an Egyptian overseer and fled to the desert. And all those years he was gone from them, marrying a foreign woman, having children by her. Until one day—she had foreseen it in a dream—he had come back to save his people.

They had waited, all of them, while Moses negotiated with Pharaoh. The pharaoh made all those promises and broke them all—no matter that the God of Israel had sent plague after plague to warn him. Not until the death of his own son did he in despair relent.

So Moses had called them together. "Hurry," he said. "We will go—before he changes his mind again."

They have come this far—even a way made for them to cross the Reed Sea. But Pharaoh must have changed his mind. The horsemen gather at the shore, and the path across the sand is open for the enemy, too. Have they come this far only to be killed in a foreign land? For a moment Miriam turns her head away. She cannot bear to look.

She turns back toward her brother Moses. He is standing there, his rod upraised. The wind has shifted so his hair blows across his face. But the people are not watching him. They are facing the sea, their faces frozen in horror and disbelief. She follows their glance, hears muffled shouts of terror from the far shore.

The walls of water have fallen forward in turbulent waves. The pursuing Egyptians—with their chariots and horses, their bright burnished armor—are being tumbled, inundated, drowned by the returning sea.

At first the Israelites are silent, aghast, scarcely believing what they see with their own eyes. Miriam glances at Moses. His face is transported, illumined as from some inner fire.

Then a shout of triumph breaks forth, and then another and another, as they realize what has happened. They are safe!

Many of the sages were convinced that God took events in the life of Israel that appeared to be evil and destructive and turned them toward the good. For example, when those who were escaping from the Egyptians reached the sea, it seemed the end for them; yet the sea opened to provide them a passageway to safety. So they celebrate the event with singing and dancing. One rabbi told a story as an example of God's turning evil into good: A woman complained that her son did not treat her as well as he should. When the case came before the judge, she saw that the judge sentenced those convicted to be beaten and imprisoned. When the woman saw how harsh the judge's sentences were, she changed her mind. When the judge asked her what complaint she had against her son, she hesitated, then said, "While I carried him in my womb, he kicked me." The judge was puzzled, "Is that all? Does he mistreat you now?" She answered, "No," for she realized that her complaint paled when compared to the punishment her son might receive. So the judge let the young man go free. Just so, God, like the mother, relents from the harshest of punishment and instead offers the people another chance. This is truly something to sing about. (*Leviticus Rabbah* 27.6)

Miriam leaps from the crowd. Once again their God has saved them! And her brother, God's agent. She might have guessed it. She grasps a timbrel in one hand and, holding her skirt, wet from the spray of the sea, in her other hand, she begins to dance, moving in dips and twirls and leaps.

"Sing to the Lord," she sings, "for he has triumphed gloriously; the horse and his rider he has thrown into the sea." And all the people raise their arms and shout for joy. *(Martha Whitmore Hickman)*

Miriam

Miriam is stricken with leprosy after she and Aaron complain about their brother, Moses.

The Story

Miriam and Aaron began to find fault with Moses. They criticized him for his Cushite wife (for he had married a Cushite woman), and they complained, 'Is Moses the only one by whom the LORD has spoken? Has he not spoken by us as well?'—though Moses was a man of great humility, the most humble man on earth. But the LORD heard them and at once said to Moses, Aaron, and Miriam, 'Go out all three of you to the Tent of Meeting.' When they went out, the LORD descended in a pillar of cloud and, standing at the entrance to the tent, he summoned Aaron and Miriam. The two of them came forward, and the LORD said,

'Listen to my words.
If he were your prophet and nothing
  more,
I would make myself known to him
  in a vision,
I would speak with him in a dream.
But my servant Moses is not such a
prophet;
of all my household he alone is faithful.
With him I speak face to face,

openly and not in riddles.
He sees the very form of the LORD.
How dare you speak against my servant
Moses?'

With his anger still hot against them, the LORD left them; and as the cloud moved from the tent, there was Miriam, her skin diseased and white as snow. When Aaron, turning towards her, saw her skin diseased, he said to Moses, 'My lord, do not make us pay the penalty of sin, foolish and wicked though we have been. Let her not be like something still-born, whose flesh is half eaten away when it comes from the womb.' So Moses cried, 'LORD, not this! Heal her, I pray.' The LORD answered, 'Suppose her father had spat in her face, would she not have to remain in disgrace for seven days? Let her be confined outside the camp for seven days and then be brought back.' So Miriam was shut out-side for seven days, and the people did not strike camp until she was brought back. After that they moved on from Hazeroth and pitched camp in the wilderness of Paran.

Comments on the Story

In the above section (Exod. 15:1-21) we saw the brief, but important, refer-ences to Miriam as a prophet and community leader. The present selection pre-

73

serves a dispute over leadership between Miriam and Aaron against Moses. Its polemical nature against Miriam probably accounts for the paucity of references to a woman who was an important force in Israel's early history. Apparently, as the three leaders competed for authority, Moses became stronger, and Miriam's ability to be a spokesperson declined.

Ostensibly, the dispute is over Moses' marriage to a Cushite woman, but the words of Miriam and Aaron betray the real reason for the argument: They find that Moses, rather than they, continues to be recognized as God's spokesperson. This problem reflects a dispute in the community. On some debatable or controversial issues, people take sides—some with Moses, and some with Miriam and Aaron. Obviously, the people who honored Moses most have preserved this account, as it is told from a point of view that favors Moses, calling him "the most humble man on earth" (v. 3).

Although the text is brief, the reference to the dispute about the Cushite woman may belie a dispute among the Israelites concerning the inclusion of certain foreigners among them. Some scholars have identified the Cushite woman with the Midianite woman Zipporah, whom Moses had married, as is known in Exodus. Others identify Cush with Ethiopia and see that Moses has married another woman. So the dispute could be that Moses has married another foreign woman (all foreign women could be suspect at times) or that this particular woman from Cush was problematic. Some scholars argue that the Cushite woman prompted the argument among Moses, Miriam, and Aaron either because she was of a different race (unlikely, since the Hebrew Bible does not appear as conscious of racial identification as is our own culture) or because she was a more wealthy, privileged person (some scholars argue that Cush, which is identified with Ethiopia, was known for its advanced society and wealth). All these possibilities can be entertained, but the reference to the Cushite woman serves primarily as the item that forces the issue about leadership.

In order that no doubt remain about the location of proper authority in the community, God speaks, specifically addressing Aaron and Miriam. The use of poetry emphasizes the importance of God's words, which indicate that Moses, alone of all people, sees God's very form. Miriam and Aaron are thus rebuked for questioning Moses.

As the angry God departs, it is Miriam who suffers for her and Aaron's questioning of Moses. She is covered with leprous sores on her skin—so devastating it is described as "white as snow." Why is Aaron spared? Some suggest that because he was a priest who could not function in a state of impurity, it would be impossible for the community to accept him or for a later community to include the narratives about him. Miriam, a woman, is more dispensable. She is a prophet, but not a priest. She has dared to question Moses. Thus, as a woman, she is singled out. Aaron has to plead with Moses to pray for her.

74

He does so, but God and Moses ignore Miriam and discuss the leprosy in a detached fashion. Miriam, still leprous, is confined outside the Israelite camp for seven days. It is a testimony to the people's respect for her that they did not move until she was able to join them.

We do not hear much else about Miriam's role in the Israelite community. It is significant, however, that even though the stories about her remain sparse, her death is recorded as the final testimony to her importance in a crucial period of Israel's experience (Num. 20:1).

Retelling the Story

Now don't get me wrong, I love my little brother. It's just that sometimes he gets to acting too big for his britches. He was bad before, but now that he's "Senior Pastor" of our church he's worse than ever. He seems to forget that it was me who came up with the name The Church of the New Israel and the Free Captives in the first place. Now tell me, could he ever have come up with such a name if he had thought about it for a year? Well, no he couldn't.

And to tell you the truth, he's not that good a preacher to begin with. Why, he talks so slow that people fall asleep between words. And not everybody likes him, no siree. There was plenty of complaining when we moved from that church basement in a nicer part of town into this trailer. Since then we've had to move around so much that people forget where to come to services. If my baby brother hadn't been so ugly to the mayor in the first place, we might have never had to leave. But now that we've moved across the river there's no going back.

When the ministry got so busy that he needed help, I thought he might pick me as an assistant pastor or something. But did he? No, he picked out seven of his buddies to be elders.

Sometimes Miriam is referred to as "Aaron's sister," rather than as "Moses' and Aaron's sister," and the rabbis were puzzled at that. Wasn't she sister to both? One of the sages explained that, though Miriam was sister to both brothers, Aaron had a special affection for her. This is demonstrated by the fact that Aaron intercedes with Moses for their sister when she is stricken with leprosy. (*Genesis Rabbah* 80.10)

When I asked him why, he said he didn't need an assistant pastor; he needed elders. I reminded him that I was his elder by several years. Then he started in telling me that I was a woman (which I already knew!) and that women were supposed to keep their heads covered and their mouths shut in church. Then he said he wouldn't tolerate a woman to exercise leadership over a man in his congregation. *His congregation?* Well, that was it for me. I told him straight out that if that was the way he felt I would just keep my wallet covered and my pocketbook shut and that he could exercise all the leadership he could pay for without my tithe. I don't pay for something I don't have any say so about.

It was about that time that this skin problem began to come on me. Red patches on my face and hands, and they just hurt like blazes. At first the doctor thought it was something terrible, but now he has decided that it's just nerves. I could have told him that to start with—that brother of mine would torment a rock til it broke out in a dread disease. Shortly after I came down with my skin problem that little brother of mine wrote me a letter saying that my affliction was the judgment of God sent down on me for opposing God's chosen, by which he meant himself. Well, that made me so mad I could just spit. But I didn't do or say anything ugly back. I just waited.

You see, for all the fussing we have done my baby brother and I depend on each other. I knew it was just a matter of time before he would come back around and things would be fine again. Just about the time my skin cleared up I heard that some of the elders he had picked were falling down on the job. Also quite a few of the other women in the congregation stopped giving their tithe when I stopped mine, and for the same reason. Though it may not be religious as such, it is a principle of life here—no taxation without representation. So the church had fallen on hard times in more than one way.

> After seven days, someone would have to examine Miriam to determine if she was clean from leprosy. But who would do the examination? It shouldn't be Moses, because he wasn't a priest. It shouldn't be Aaron, because—though he was a priest—he was also a relative. So the rabbis say that God did the examination and that the Shekhinah, the presence of God, waited until she could travel with them before moving the people on. (*Leviticus Rabbah* 15.8)

It wasn't too long before my little brother called up and asked if I would consider coming back to the church. I told him I would, if he needed an assistant pastor. He said he did, and I didn't remind him of any of the terrible things he had said to me before about women exercising authority and such. I just asked how often did he think I would get to preach, and he said we would talk about that. Then he told me that he assumed that I would start up giving my tithe again, and I told him we would talk about that, too. Then he said he was glad we were talking again, and I told him I was, too.

You see, I never doubted that my baby brother was hand-picked by God for something important. I just didn't want him questioning that I was called just like him. Besides, I love him, even if he does get too big for his britches every now and again. But then, who doesn't? *(Michael E. Williams)*

JOSHUA 2:1-24; 6:1-2, 25

Rahab

A prostitute hides and protects the Israelite spies when they enter the land of Canaan and is rewarded for her efforts.

The Story

Joshua son of Nun sent out two spies secretly from Shittim with orders to reconnoitre the land and especially Jericho. The two men set off and came to the house of a prostitute named Rahab to spend the night there. When it was reported to the king of Jericho that some Israelites had arrived that night to explore the country, he sent word to Rahab: 'Bring out the men who have come to you and are now in your house, for they have come to spy out the whole country.' The woman, who had taken the two men and hidden them, replied, 'True, the men did come to me, but I did not know where they came from; and at nightfall when it was time to shut the gate, they had gone. I do not know where they were going, but if you hurry after them you may overtake them.' In fact, she had brought them up on to the roof and concealed them among the stalks of flax which she had laid out there in rows. The messengers went in pursuit of them in the direction of the fords of the Jordan, and as soon as they had gone out the gate was closed.

The men had not yet settled down, when Rahab came up to them on the roof, and said, 'I know that the LORD has given the land to you; terror of you has fallen upon us, and the whole country is panic-stricken. We have heard how the LORD dried up the waters of the Red Sea before you when you came out of Egypt, and what you did to Sihon and Og, the two Amorite kings beyond the Jordan, for you destroyed them. When we heard this, our courage failed; your coming has left no spirit in any of us; for the LORD your God is God in heaven above and on earth below. Swear to me by the LORD that you will keep faith with my family, as I have kept faith with you. Give me a token of good faith; promise that you will spare the lives of my father and mother, my brothers and sisters, and all who belong to them, and preserve us from death.' The men replied, 'Our lives for yours, so long as you do not betray our business. When the LORD gives us the country, we shall deal loyally and faithfully by you.'

She then let them down through a window by a rope; for the house where she lived was on an angle of the wall. 'Make for the hills,' she said, 'or the pursuers will come upon you. Hide there for three days until they return; then go on your way.' The men warned her that, unless she did what they told her, they would be free from the oath she had made them take. 'When we invade the

77

land,' they said, 'you must fasten this strand of scarlet cord in the window through which you have lowered us, and get everybody together here inside the house, your father and mother, your brothers, and all your family. Should anybody go out of doors into the street, his blood will be on his own head; we shall be free of the oath. But if a hand is laid on anyone who stays indoors with you, his blood be on our heads! Remember too that, if you betray our business, then we shall be free of the oath you have made us take.' 'It shall be as you say,' she replied, and sent them on their way. When they had gone, she fastened the strand of scarlet cord in the window.

The men made their way into the hills and stayed there for three days until the pursuers returned. They had searched all along the road, but had not found them. The two men then came down from the hills and crossed the river. When they joined up with Joshua son of Nun, they reported all that had happened to them. 'The LORD has delivered the whole country into our hands,' they said; 'the inhabitants are all panic-stricken at our approach.'

Jericho was bolted and barred against the Israelites; no one could go out or in. The LORD said to Joshua, 'See, I am delivering Jericho, its king, and his warriors into your hands.' . . .

Thus Joshua spared the lives of Rahab the prostitute, her household, and all who belonged to her, because she had hidden the men whom Joshua had sent to reconnoitre Jericho; she and her family settled permanently among the Israelites.

Comments on the Story

The story of Rahab and Joshua's spies comes at the beginning of the book of Joshua, which deals with Israel's entrance into the land of Canaan. It reflects upon Israel's struggles against a cunning, enormous, and oppressive enemy. Throughout the book, the Israelites suffer because of the disobedience of some of those among them, but they also witness God's abounding graciousness: God fights for them against their enemies. It is not merely a struggle for territory and control but, like the story of the Exodus, is rooted in a vision of justice and freedom from tyrants. The land of the promise is also to be the land of covenantal fidelity, not the land dominated by the whims of the Canaanite kings.

Joshua, Moses' successor, plans to gain a foothold in central Canaan at Jericho. The necessity of sending spies alerts the reader to the formidable task. Joshua's men decide to spend the night at the house of the prostitute Rahab, but their intentions are not explained. This gap enables the reader to consider various possibilities. Could the spies, who are on a mission for Joshua, become sidetracked by engaging in intercourse with a prostitute? Would this sin jeopardize the community? Could she and her compatriots harm them? Are they there simply to obtain information about the town from someone who is accessible? None of these questions is answered, but because they can be entertained, the spies' safety in the end is all the more surprising.

Almost immediately after the spies come to Rahab's house, their presence becomes known in the larger community, perhaps pointing to their poor judgment in going there. The king inquires of Rahab. He understands the spies' mission: The entire land, not only Jericho, is threatened by the Israelite presence. How will Rahab respond? The reader may assume the spies are still present; the narrator has not revealed they have departed. Rahab, a Canaanite woman and a prostitute, might be expected to tell the king's messenger where they are. Only after the tension builds does the reader discover her surprising response: She says that the men have departed. It still may be the case that she is a loyal subject to the king because she tells the king's representatives that they may be able to pursue and overtake the men. The readers must still wonder about the spies' safety because the narrator has not revealed their whereabouts.

Only after this suspenseful incident does the narrator specify that the spies are really being hidden by Rahab's ingenuity and that she risked lying to the king's men in order to save Joshua's spies. The care with which she hid them is noted: "She had brought them up onto the roof and concealed them among the stalks of flax which she had laid out there in rows" (v. 6). The reader continues to receive more information about the safety of the spies as the narrator relates that in fact the kings' men follow Rahab's advice and leave the city to pursue them. Joshua's soldiers are out of immediate danger.

After receiving the surprising information that this Canaanite woman lied in order to protect Israelites, the reader learns that the woman has great faith—faith in the God of Israel! Rahab comes to check on the men, even before they have settled down. This information shows the degree to which Rahab is concerned because she tends to them immediately despite the danger. Rahab's advice to the king's messengers to leave the premises in order to quickly pursue the spies saves their lives. If, for example, the messengers searched her home, they would have found the unhidden men. When Rahab speaks she perceives the consequences of their mission: The LORD has given the land to the Israelites. Her reference to the people's being "panic-stricken" is the type of language that indicates that the LORD is fighting for the Israelites, stressing that the Israelites have victory because of God's intervention, and not because of their own merit or skill in warfare. She recites the message of the Exodus, which forms the paradigm for the Israelite success over the Amorite kings and positions them for success in Canaan. Her recital of faith is most striking: "The LORD your God is God in heaven above and on earth below" (v. 11). In essence, she is swearing loyalty to the God of Israel. Thus she asks that she and her family be spared when Joshua takes Jericho in battle. The men agree. Appropriately, some commentators see her as representative of the Canaanite peasants who joined the Israelites in their movement to redefine the government (and social system and religion) of Canaan.

Rahab continues to assist Joshua's men by allowing them to escape the city stealthily and by suggesting the location and duration of his hiding. Joshua's men respond by explaining how she and her family's lives will be saved in Jericho if she marks her house with a red cord, stressing that it is her responsibility to see that the home is so designated. These directions are given, presumably, because of the ravages and confusion of battle. When the men return to Joshua, they echo Rahab's words about God's deliverance. Joshua is now poised to take Jericho because of the success of the spies' mission.

The reader has learned from this account that the city of Jericho is walled, and chapter 6 begins with a reminder of this formidable obstacle. The famous account of the destruction of the city of Jericho stresses the miraculous and the religious (the priests and peoples' procession around the city, the blasts of the rams' horns, the walls falling down) in order to underscore that it was God's victory. As the selected Scripture passage makes clear, just as God was faithful to Israel, so also the Israelites were faithful to Rahab and her family. Rahab had an important role in the fulfillment of God's plan for Israel's success in Canaan. At the end of this account, she is part of the people of Israel as well.

Retelling the Story

It is usually a terrifying thing to lie to the authorities. So it was no wonder that her fingers trembled behind her back as the young woman told the soldiers her story. Yes, the strangers had been there. She had no idea where they were from. They had gone by the time everything was closing that evening. She had no idea where they were going, though they had mentioned something about a train leaving the city by midnight, but she had not heard from which station they would depart.

The sages tell that when Rahab hid the spies in her house she was not fully conscious of what she was doing. In other words, she knew that she was doing the spies a favor, but she did not realize that her good deed was for God, as well. But God counted it as if she was fully conscious of what she was doing and did it in accordance with the divine will. (*Numbers Rabbah* 8.9)

As she spoke these words, for an instant she thought she could almost hear the breathing of her guests, hidden away in the attic. She knew that was ridiculous, impossible that anyone could hear even the restless stirring of a person from that distance. *It is just my fear getting the better of me,* she attempted to assure herself, and there was no indication that the officers doubted her word.

After all, they had no reason to question her story. Many times in the past they had allowed her to continue her work, the oldest profession, after only a perfunctory examination. That is where she learned the great advantage of the bold lie. After all, they had an understanding, which made the situation like a little drama only they knew they were enacting. "I am simply an 'entertainer,'" she was to say. The officers would ask to examine her "entertainment." Then they would have their pick of the young women who "entertained" in her establishment. Once the authorities were sufficiently "entertained" (at no cost to them, of course), she would be protected from any unnecessary interruption of business.

Her present situation was very different. She and the officers had no understanding about hiding Jews. She knew that if they really even suspected her of harboring "enemies of the state" she would have no protection. In fact, she would share the fate of those with whom she shared her rooms. Officially no one knew what everyone really knew—the fate was a trip to a concentration camp, then death.

Wouldn't the handsome officers come in for a short while and take advantage of the hospitality of her house? She employed many beautiful and skillful "entertainers," one of whom would certainly please even the most selective young man. And these were obviously officers with only the finest taste in "entertainment." She had found that flattery was a fail-proof diversion with conscripts into military service. They already liked to think they looked irresistible in their uniforms.

The glint in their eyes and the hint of a smile that creased each man's mouth assured her that her strategy had worked again. They would take their pleasure and take her message back to their unit commander. From there it would travel up to the highest seat of power in the land. Soldiers would spend the night combing the railroad stations and departing trains, while she had already secured her "guests'" passage on a boat. By the time the soldiers gave up their search, the Jews would be out of danger.

> Many of the rabbis were so impressed by the risks Rahab took in order to hide the spies that they suggest she was not really a harlot. Rather, some claim she was simply an innkeeper, while others say she was a dealer in cosmetics and perfumes. However she earned her living, the sages say that her good deed was so appreciated by God and the people that even if there were two hundred in her family, all of them were brought out of Jericho. Some go so far as to say that if that large household were related to two hundred other families, they would all escape, since the story says that all her "families" were brought out. (*Ruth Rabbah* 2.1)

After the officers and her "guests" were gone she sat up long into the night, pondering why she was willing to risk everything for the Jewish families who passed through her house. She was no hausfrau that she should care about families, nor was she a churchgoer. In fact, most of the religious people of the city condemned her and her house of "entertainment." As with the concentration camps, no one officially knew of her business, yet everyone seemed to know of her activity. She had become prosperous by fulfilling the illicit yearnings of others.

She was not even a "good" person. She was not "respectable." Yet when she saw the "good, respectable" people of her country rounding up families to send to their death simply because they were Jewish, she just could not go along. If this is what it meant to be respectable and a good person, she would settle for a less noble path, saving innocent lives. If the authorities caught her, she knew that she would lose all she had worked to gain. Who knows, perhaps the God of the Jews was merciful, as they claimed. Perhaps she would be considered one of the "righteous among the nations," as many of her guests suggested. She would leave that up to the God who had created them and her, and even the good, respectable people who were their persecutors.

It is, indeed, a terrifying thing to lie to the authorities. Worse still is to stand by and see innocent people sent to their deaths victims of a blind hatred that paraded as patriotism, respectability, and even faith. *(Michael E. Williams)*

While the rabbis view Israel as God's chosen people, they also recognize that there are those among many nations and people whom God accepts and loves. These are called "the righteous among the nations." Rahab is a prototype of one of the righteous people. Though not of Israel, she—consciously or unconsciously—lives in a way that is pleasing to God. Today at Yad Vashem, the museum in Jerusalem that holds some of the memories of the Holocaust, there is a path called the walkway of the righteous among the nations. It is lined with plaques bearing the names of Gentiles who assisted Jews to escape from the clutches of Hitler's "final solution." (*Ecclesiastes Rabbah* 5.11[1])

JUDGES 4:1-24

Deborah

Deborah, a judge among the people, assists in a military victory but tells the general that he will not receive credit for it; a woman will.

The Story

After Ehud's death the Israelites once again did what was wrong in the eyes of the LORD, and he sold them into the power of Jabin, the Canaanite king who ruled in Hazor. The commander of his forces was Sisera, who lived in Harosheth-of-the-Gentiles. The Israelites cried to the LORD for help, because Sisera with his nine hundred iron-clad chariots had oppressed Israel harshly for twenty years.

At that time Deborah wife of Lappidoth, a prophetess, was judge in Israel. It was her custom to sit under the Palm Tree of Deborah between Ramah and Bethel in the hill-country of Ephraim, and Israelites seeking a judgment went up to her. She sent for Barak son of Abinoam from Kedesh in Naphtali and said to him, 'This is the command of the LORD the God of Israel: Go and lead out ten thousand men from Naphtali and Zebulun and bring them with you to Mount Tabor. I shall draw out to you at the wadi Kishon Jabin's commander Sisera, along with his chariots and troops, and deliver him into your power.' Barak answered, 'If you go with me, I shall go, but if you will not go, neither shall I.' 'Certainly I shall go with you,' she said, 'but this venture will bring you no glory, because the LORD will leave Sisera to fall into the hands of a woman.' Deborah set off with Barak and went to Kedesh. Barak mustered Zebulun and Naphtali to Kedesh and marched up with ten thousand followers; Deborah went up with him.

Now Heber the Kenite had parted company with the Kenites, the descendants of Hobab, Moses' brother-in-law, and he had pitched his tent at Elon-bezaanannim near Kedesh.

When it was reported to Sisera that Barak son of Abinoam had gone up to Mount Tabor, he mustered all nine hundred of his iron-clad chariots, along with all the troops he had, and marched from Harosheth-of-the-Gentiles to the wadi Kishon. Deborah said to Barak, 'Up! This day the LORD is to give Sisera into your hands. See, the LORD has marched out at your head!' Barak came down from Mount Tabor with ten thousand men at his back, and the LORD threw Sisera and all his chariots and army into panic-striken rout before Barak's onslaught; Sisera himself dismounted from his chariot and fled on foot. Barak pursued the chariots and the troops as far as Harosheth, and the whole army was put to the sword; not a man was left alive.

Meanwhile Sisera fled on foot to the

tent of Jael wife of Heber the Kenite, because King Jabin of Hazor and the household of Heber the Kenite were on friendly terms. Jael came out to greet Sisera and said, 'Come in, my lord, come in here; do not be afraid.' He went into the tent, and she covered him with a rug. He said to her, 'Give me some water to drink, for I am thirsty,' She opened a skin of milk, gave him a drink, and covered him again. He said to her, 'Stand at the tent door, and if anyone comes and asks if there is a man here, say "No." ' But as Sisera lay fast asleep through exhaustion Jael took a tent-peg, picked up a mallet, and, creeping up to him, drove the peg into his temple, so that it went down into the ground, and Sisera died. When Barak came by in pursuit of Sisera, Jael went out to meet him. 'Come,' she said, 'I shall show you the man you are looking for.' He went in with her, and there was Sisera lying dead with the tent-peg in his temple. That day God gave victory to the Israelites over King Jabin of Canaan, and they pressed home their attacks upon him until he was destroyed.

Comments on the Story

The book of Judges employs a repeated literary pattern of sin, punishment, crying out to God, and salvation in order to underscore Israel's utter dependence on God. When Israel sins, Canaanites oppress them; when they appeal to God, God answers by sending a judge who is victorious over the oppressor. In this lectionary selection, Deborah, with the assistance of her compatriot Barak and the foreigner Jael, acts as God's agent to bring deliverance from an intractable enemy: the king of Hazor and his general Sisera.

The strength of the enemy is indicated by the nine hundred chariots (a weapon the Israelites did not possess) as well as the length of time they had oppressed Israel—twenty years. The narrator indicates that Deborah was a prophet and judge in Israel. As prophet, she acts as God's spokesperson; as judge she acts as arbiter in disputes and, more important, as a military leader. As God's spokesperson, she commands Barak to ready his troops because salvation is at hand. Just as in the paradigmatic Exodus story, here salvation refers to God's deliverance of the community from political oppression. By using the direct address for Deborah, the narrator underscores her authority and strength. She tells Barak directly of God's command and is specific in her directions for Barak's action. In contrast to Deborah's unquestioned confidence in God's plan, Barak wavers. After being promised that God will give him victory, he insists that Deborah accompany him. Deborah agrees, but introduces a new detail of the victory: "The LORD will leave Sisera to fall into the hands of a woman" (v. 9). The reader would assume that the woman is Deborah, but the narrator builds this expectation only to surprise the reader with the appearance of Jael. We are not told of Barak's motivation for requesting the accompaniment of Deborah. Did she have the reputation of being a great commander, as were the other judges of Israel? The silence is particularly mystifying, given that she was a woman and we have little evidence of women as soldiers or military leaders. Unfortunately, there is no further explanation.

Using the language typical of battle wherein the LORD fights for Israel, Deborah, still acting as God's spokesperson and military advisor to Barak, states that the enemy is defeated because the LORD is the true commander. Although Deborah is not described as a soldier, Barak does not act until she tells him to move. After the enemy soldiers are put into a "panic-stricken rout" by God, Barak's troops are successful. The enemy is defeated—all except Sisera, who escapes.

The narrator has told an engaging account and has now introduced a puzzle. The reader may have expected that Deborah would personally defeat Sisera. Why has he escaped? Now the apparent digression concerning Heber the Kenite (v. 11) becomes clear. His wife, Jael, now encounters Sisera, and Sisera understandably believes she will befriend him because her husband is an ally of his people. Indeed, she is solicitous of him, even providing him with more than he requests. It is arresting, therefore, that when he commands her to guard the tent entrance while he sleeps, she instead kills him with a makeshift weapon of a tent peg and a mallet.

A poem reciting the account of the victory is included here as well. Many scholars suggest that it is one of the oldest texts of the Hebrew Bible. It is a tribute to the importance of Deborah in Israel's memory that she is credited with this song. This poem stresses themes that are central not only to the prose account of Deborah, but also to the entire book of Judges. Verses 1-11 describe the terror inflicted upon the Israelites by the Canaanites and the Lord's victories on behalf of Israel. Deborah is singled out as a "mother" of Israel; in this context the reference is to the champion of the country's cause against oppression. Deborah's military role is recalled in verses 12-18, which highlight her actions as the director of the battle and single out the tribes who either supported or abandoned her and Barak. Verses 19-23 credit God for the victory, and using language typical of theophany in the Hebrew Bible, the stars and the Wadi Kishon fight against Sisera. Verses 24-27 dramatically credit Jael, the foreign woman, for Sisera's death. Jael is contrasted with the description of Sisera's mother and the mother's servants. A humble woman has slain Sisera, yet his privileged mother and other women await what they think will be his victorious return with the spoils of war. The poem appropriately ends with the description of the enemy women who are yet uninformed of the defeat of their men. The reversal has occurred. The tyrants can no longer oppress because of the LORD's victory through the crucial women participants: Deborah and Jael.

Retelling the Story

Women are gentle, they said. Women are nurturers and unused to killing and war. Make a woman a judge, and it will mean the end of battle and siege, an end of bloodshed for honor and spoils. Some meant it as a prohibition, hoping that no woman would ever be judge, much less a military leader. Others, hoping for a time when war would end, meant it as a compliment. All were mistaken.

Deborah was tough. She would taunt the generals, saying, "If you think the hardships of military life are harsh, then you should carry a small dog inside your body for nine months, then let him climb out through your nostril. Anyone who can endure birth can endure anything." Needless to say, the generals didn't take kindly to her.

Now she was a judge. To tell the truth, she wasn't even sure how it happened. This strange and unpredictable God the Israelites followed was full of surprises. She guessed that her judicial position was just God's latest shock treatment. She took the job seriously, though. Every day, except the Sabbath, she would sit under her palm tree between Ramah and Bethel, judging the cases brought before her by the people. At first, many of the men refused to have cases heard in her court, for fear she would favor women or that she would be overly emotional in her judgments.

> When the sages speak of Esther and Mordecai as being chosen just for the occasion recounted in the book named for Esther, they list others chosen for a particular moment in history. Among those recounted is Deborah. While the rabbis do not go on to say so, it would seem that God chooses the right person for the job, regardless of gender. (*Esther Rabbah* 5.4)

Deborah favored no one, and she showed so little emotion in her judgments that some began to compare her to the tree under which she sat. Crowds would gather in her open-air courtroom to see justice that was truly just. Her decisions were impartial, giving credit where credit was due and issuing punishment where punishment was deserved. Her decisions were swayed by neither power nor money nor gender.

That is why no one was surprised when she sent for Barak and told him where and how he was to fight his enemy, Sisera. Barak thought he had Deborah where he wanted her. "If you know so much about military strategy, why don't you just come with me?" They nearly had to pick Barak up off the ground when she replied, "That's just what I was hoping you would ask." Now, even Barak was shocked when she told him that, though the battle would be his, he would receive no credit for the victory, since God will let the opposing general be taken by a woman.

Everyone knew that this was not just a rhetorical exercise coming from Deborah. It might as well have issued from the mouth of God. She stood and watched as the soldiers of Barak looked in vain among the slaughtered for the body of Sisera. She knew their search was useless. Call it judgment; call it intuition; call it what you like. She knew what would happen as surely as if she had written the script herself, and she would not soft-pedal that knowledge for any general.

> There was debate among the rabbis concerning which judges the writer had in mind when the text says that the people did not listen to their judges (Judg. 2:17). Three rabbis list judges whose wisdom was ignored. Deborah is on two of the three lists. (*Ruth Rabbah* 1.1)

As she left the field of battle that day, above the noise of victory celebrations and far beyond the moans and cries of the dying she thought she could hear the insistent tap, tap, tap of a mallet striking honor out of the trembling hands of Barak. Somewhere in the distance, a tent peg entered the ground and set free a song in the throats of women:

> "Champions there were none,
> none left in Israel,
> until you, Deborah, arose,
> arose as a mother in Israel."
> *(Michael E. Williams)*

87

Jephthah's Daughter

An outcast become leader promises to sacrifice whatever meets him upon his return home in exchange for victory. Little does he know it will be his daughter.

The Story

The time came when the Ammonites launched an offensive against Israel and, when the fighting began, the elders of Gilead went to fetch Jephthah from the land of Tob. 'Come and be our commander so that we can fight the Ammonites,' they said to him. But Jephthah answered, 'You drove me from my father's house in hatred. Why come to me now when you are in trouble?' 'It is because of that,' they replied, 'that we have turned to you now. Come with us, fight the Ammonites, and become head over all the inhabitants of Gilead.' Jephthah said to them, 'If you ask me back to fight the Ammonites and if the LORD delivers them into my hands, then I must become your head.' The Gilead elders said to him, 'We swear by the LORD, who will be witness between us, that we will do what you say.' Jephthah then went with the elders of Gilead, and the people made him their head and commander. And at Mizpah, in the presence of the LORD, Jephthah repeated the terms he had laid down. . . .

Then the spirit of the LORD came upon Jephthah, who passed through Gilead and Manasseh, by Mizpah of Gilead, and from Mizpah over to the Ammonites. Jephthah made this vow to the LORD: 'If you will deliver the Ammonites into my hands, then the first creature that comes out of the door of my house to meet me when I return from them safely shall be the LORD's; I shall offer that as a whole-offering.'

So Jephthah crossed over to attack the Ammonites, and the LORD delivered them into his hands. He routed them with very great slaughter all the way from Aroer to near Minnith, taking twenty towns, and as far as Abel-keramim. Thus Ammon was subdued by Israel.

When Jephthah arrived home in Mizpah, it was his daughter who came out to meet him with tambourines and dancing. She was his only child; apart from her he had neither son nor daughter.

At the sight of her, he tore his clothes and said, 'Oh, my daughter, you have broken my heart! Such calamity you have brought on me! I have made a vow to the LORD and I cannot go back on it.'

She replied, 'Father, since you have made a vow to the LORD, do to me as your vow demands, now that the LORD has avenged you on the Ammonites, your enemies. But, father, grant me this one favour: spare me for two months, that I may roam the hills with my companions and mourn that I must die a virgin.' 'Go,' he said, and he let her depart for two months. She went with her companions and mourned her virginity on the hills. At the end of two months she came back to her father, and he fulfilled the vow he had made; she died a virgin. It became a tradition that the daughters of Israel should go year by year and commemorate for four days the daughter of Jephthah the Gileadite.

Comments on the Story

The setting of this text is the repeated struggle of the Israelites, and especially the people of the region of Gilead, with the Ammonites. In their desperate straits, the Gileadites turn to Jephthah, a warrior with a mixed reputation. The son of a prostitute, his character is questioned; indeed, his half brothers drive him away from home and rebuke him. While in exile, Jephthah forms a guerrilla army with other disenfranchised and disgruntled men. Eventually, he will bring Gilead victory, but only at the terrible cost of the loss of his daughter's life by his own hand.

Although the narrator does not state specifically why the elders of Gilead turn to him when facing the Ammonite offensive, the reader may assume it is because of his reputation as a guerrilla leader. Given his past treatment, Jephthah questions their sincerity, and though they offer to make him their leader, he continues to insist. Jephthah sets the terms precisely: If the Lord gives him victory, then they must make him their leader. They assent. Curiously, the Gileadites make him their head even before he fights for them and before victory is assured. This premature action sets the stage for the thoughtless and unnecessary vow that Jephthah will take, which has tragic consequences.

Jephthah first acts not as a warrior, but as a diplomat, attempting to solve the dispute with the Ammonites by persuasion. He recites Israel's past history concerning the region and how Israel never took Ammonite territory. Only when the Israelites were refused passage in the region did the LORD give them victory—including lands that the Ammonites are now claiming. In his recital, Jephthah's theology appears confusing. On the one hand, he holds that local gods are responsible for each nation's victories. For example, he claims that Kemosh gives the Ammonites their land (in other texts, Milcom, rather than Kemosh, is identified as Ammon's god). On the other hand, Jephthah states, "The LORD who is judge will decide this day between the Israelites and the Ammonites" (v. 27), appealing to a more powerful deity.

As is the case with other judges who fight for Israel, the spirit of the LORD descends upon Jephthah so that he will have victory. Without provocation or explanation, Jephthah makes a vow to the LORD that upon receiving victory he will sacrifice whatever or whomever he first sees upon returning home. It would be hard to imagine a more thoughtless vow. Other judges' victories are not prompted by such vows; they do not need to bargain for the LORD's presence. Indeed, there is no confirmation that this vow was necessary or acceptable to God. Human sacrifice, although sometimes practiced in Israel, was repeatedly condemned. Jephthah, however, obviously considered it to be acceptable, as the possibility that a human being would first greet him would be readily apparent.

When Jephthah's victory is described, the narrator makes clear that it was due to the LORD's deliverance; the vow is given neither reference nor credence. Despite Jephthah's hesitancy, as reflected in his use of the vow, the LORD gives him an extensive and complete victory.

The arresting nature of the vow reaches its climax in verse 34. Not only is it a human being who greets Jephthah, but it is his own daughter. The foolishness and lack of faith of the father is contrasted with the innocence of the daughter: she comes out dancing with tambourines. Only after seeing this tragic development of the narrative does the reader learn the more pathetic result of Jephthah's vow. Since he has no other offspring, the daughter's death will be the end of his family. Jephthah's reaction when he sees his daughter is as thoughtless as his vow. He never entertains the idea of an alternate sacrifice. Given that human sacrifice was continually chastised in Israel, the reader would know how arresting his outrageous behavior truly was. In addition, he never considers retracting the vow, an action that has precedence in the story of Saul and Jonathan (1 Sam. 14). He rends his garments, a sign of mourning, upon seeing his daughter, and blames her for his grief, claiming he cannot deny his vow.

The daughter's response moves us because of her continued innocence and powerlessness. She does not cry out or challenge her father. Her final request serves to reinforce the injustice done to her. She requests two months time to mourn her virginity—a reference to the fact that she will die childless, considered a great burden of suffering. It is appropriate that she asks to complete her mourning with her female companions (the word for "companions," *reotay,* refers to girls or women only)—those who can best appreciate the pain she is feeling. It is those unnamed women and their successive generations who remain faithful to this unnamed daughter. In contrast to Jephthah, who obliterates his daughter's and his own progeny, the women remember her every year in a four-day ceremony.

Retelling the Story

Jephthah bade his wife and firstborn daughter, Sheilah, goodbye. The little girl laughed to see her father go, dressed in such strange clothes, the uniform of a commander. For years he was gone. The little girl with the laughing eyes grew older. Now there was a sureness in her step. She held her head high, for her father was a great warrior, chief of all the people of Gilead, commander of a huge army.

Jephthah did not want to make war on the Ammonites. He hoped all would be resolved peacefully. But the Ammonite king would not listen to his messengers. The battles must be fought.

The army marched through Gilead and Manasseh and over to the land of the Ammonite. As they marched, Jephthah knew his men were outnumbered. His soldiers were young, not well trained. They didn't know the land; he feared they would all be killed. He looked for guidance, for wisdom. He would pray; he would promise.

> Often we think of making a vow to God to receive something in return. But the rabbis remind us that many make vows and lose instead of gain. They name Jephthah as one who vowed and lost. (*Genesis Rabbah* 70.4)

"Dear God," he whispered, "deliver the Ammonites to our hands. Help us in our fight. What do I have that is worthy to sacrifice to you for this? My life is in your hands. I solemnly vow that if we are victorious, whatever I first see at the door when I come home is yours, forever."

The battles raged.

At home the young girl's thoughts turned to her father. Surely he would be home soon. Surely he would return a hero. Surely he would hold her in his arms.

The battles continued. Men were wounded. Men died. The blood ran from the soldiers and soaked into the earth. At last, the Ammonites were defeated. Those who could fled. Jephthah's army was now a small, ragged band. They rested, buried their dead, treated their wounds.

> The sages suggest that Jephthah's vow was completely inappropriate, since he had no idea who would meet him first on his return home. So God responded in an inappropriate manner by having Jephthah's daughter be the first to encounter him. That does not mean, however, that God expected Jephthah to keep his vow. The rabbis disagree on what should have been Jephthah's response, whether, for example, to simply substitute an offering of goods in place of his daughter. Others hold that no offering was necessary, since the vow was so outrageous to begin with. They all agree, though, that God never requires human sacrifice. (*Genesis Rabbah* 60.3)

Jephthah journeyed home. Messengers preceded him. "Jephthah's army was victorious! The hero returns!"

The great commander was weary. He longed for the comfort of his family. He remembered his promise. With trepidation he wondered what would greet him first at the door: His old dog? A new young pup? He made his way through the woods and past the town. Ahead he saw his house. He began to run.

Looking out the window, Sheilah saw her father. He was here! She threw open the door and rushed toward his arms.

"No," he gasped. "Go back!"

But it was too late. Stunned, she stopped in her tracks. Her face fell as she saw his grief.

He gathered her into his embrace, weeping. "I have made a vow," he told her. "The first thing I see coming through the door I must sacrifice. You, my dearest, came to greet me. I cannot retract my promise."

She asked for two months in which to grieve, two months in which to live. This he granted to her. Why then had she been born, she wondered, to have a grave for a bridegroom? Why this sacrifice? Why? There were no answers, but she knew what she must do.

When the two months had passed, she returned from the hills. Jephthah made good his vow. A more difficult deed he had never done. A braver maiden he had never known.

To this day the women of Israel remember Sheilah, daughter of Jephthah. They remember her bravery and her sacrifice. From the highest mountains to the desert sands, they sing words of praise and cry rivers of tears. (Betty Lehrman)

The rabbis put the responsibility for the death of Jephthah's daughter on her father and the priest Phineas. They say that Jephthah was too proud to go to Phineas and ask that he be released from his vow. And Phineas was too proud to go to Jephthah on his own and release him. So the blood of the young woman was on both their heads, according to the sages. They go on the describe Jephthah's punishment for keeping his cruel vow, saying that he died by having his arms and legs fall off one at a time. In addition, it is told that each limb was buried right where it fell. (Ecclesiastes Rabbah 10.13[1])

93

Samson's Mother

A mother recieves word from a messenger of God that her son will be a Nazarite, but is not informed of the heartache he will bring to her and to others.

The Story

Once more the Israelites did what was wrong in the eyes of the LORD, and he delivered them into the hands of the Philistines for forty years.

There was a certain man from Zorah of the tribe of Dan whose name was Manoah and whose wife was barren; she had no child. The angel of the LORD appeared to her and said, "Though you are barren and have no child, you will conceive and give birth to a son. Now be careful to drink no wine or strong drink, and to eat no forbidden food. You will conceive and give birth to a son, and no razor must touch his head, for the boy is to be a Nazirite, consecrated to God from birth. He will strike the first blow for Israel's freedom from the power of the Philistines."

The woman went and told her husband, 'A man of God came to me,' she said to him; 'his appearance was that of an angel of God, most terrible to see. I did not ask him where he came from, nor did he tell me his name, but he said to me, "You are going to conceive and give birth to a son. From now on drink no wine or strong drink and eat no forbidden food, for the boy is to be a Nazarite, consecrated to God from his birth to the day of his death." '

Manoah prayed to the LORD, 'If it is pleasing to you, Lord, let the man of God whom you sent come again to tell us what we are to do for the boy that is to be born.' God heard Manoah's prayer, and the angel of God came again to the woman, as she was sitting in the field. Her husband not being with her, the woman ran quickly and said to him, 'The man who came to me the other day has appeared to me again.' Manoah went with her at once and approached the man and said, 'Are you the man who talked with my wife?' 'Yes,' he replied, 'I am.' 'Now when your words come true,' Manoah said, 'what kind of boy will he be and what will he do?' The angel of the LORD answered, 'Your wife must be careful to do all that I told her: she must not taste anything that comes from the vine; she must drink no wine or strong drink, and she must eat no forbidden food. She must do whatever I say.'

Manoah said to the angel of the LORD, 'May we urge you to stay? Let us prepare a young goat for you.' The angel replied, 'Though you urge me to stay, I shall not eat your food; but prepare a whole-offering if you will, and offer that to the LORD.' Manoah did not

95

know that he was the angel of the L<small>ORD</small>, and said to him, 'What is your name? For we shall want to honor you when your words come true.' The angel of the L<small>ORD</small> said to him, 'How can you ask my name? It is a name of wonder.' Manoah took a young goat with the proper grain-offering, and offered it on the rock to the L<small>ORD</small>, to him whose works are full of wonder. While Manoah and his wife were watching, the flame went up from the altar towards heaven, and the angel of the L<small>ORD</small> ascended in the flame. Seeing this, Manoah and his wife fell face downward to the ground.

The angel of the L<small>ORD</small> did not appear again to Manoah and his wife. When Manoah realized that it had been the angel of the L<small>ORD</small>, he said to his wife, 'We are doomed to die, for we have seen God.' But she replied, 'If the L<small>ORD</small> had wanted to kill us, he would not have accepted a whole-offering and a grain-offering at our hands; he would not now have let us see and hear all this.'

The woman gave birth to a son and named him Samson. The boy grew up in Mahaneh-dan between Zorah and Eshtaol, and the L<small>ORD</small> blessed him and the spirit of the L<small>ORD</small> began to move him.

Comments on the Story

The narrative of Manoah's wife is included not only because she is the mother of a tragic hero, Samson, but also because of her faith and loyalty to God. In contrast to her husband, she recognizes God's messenger and believes in the revelation. In contrast to her son, she strictly obeys the laws and customs required of those dedicated to the L<small>ORD</small>, the Nazirites.

The context of the revelation to Manoah's wife is the Philistine oppression of the Israelites. Philistine hegemony of the sea coast was a serious problem extending from the time of the judges to the time of David. As is done throughout the book of Judges, the introduction to this account shows that the oppression is God's punishment for Israel's sin. Many scholars see these kinds of theological statements coming from the hand of the Deuteronomic school. Writing their first and second editions of their work in the seventh and sixth centuries B.C.E., these authors were warning the Southern Kingdom of Judah to repent and learn from the lessons of Israel's failure in the past.

As the account of Manoah's wife begins, the reader learns that she has been barren, and an angel appears to announce that she will have a son. As occurs with Sarah, Rebekah, and Hannah, the announcement of a son to be born to a previously barren woman indicates God's special designs for the boy. In this case, the plan is unique because not only will the son have a role in Israel's history—in this case deliverance from the Philistines—but also because he is consecrated to God as a Nazirite. Nazirites were to live an especially holy life for a designated period of time. They were to refrain from drinking wine, from touching the dead, and from cutting their hair. It is particularly noteworthy that this child is to be considered a Nazirite from the time he is born. According to the description of the Nazirites in Numbers 6, one became a Nazarite by one's vow. Because of the unusual nature of the child's dedication, his mother is included in the regimen. She, too, must follow the law of the Nazirite.

Manoah's wife recognizes that the messenger is from God and relates her experience to her husband. Because she specifies that she did not ask his name or origin, the reader understands that she accepted the messenger's word without doubt. In retelling the messenger's instructions to her husband, she accurately quotes him—with one exception. She states that the boy is to be a Nazirite "to the day of his death," in contrast to the angel's word, which did not specify the length of time the boy would be consecrated. The narrator may have intentionally included this remark here because she appears unknowingly prescient; Samson dies prematurely and never offers the customary sacrifice that Nazirites used to mark the end of their service.

In contrast to his wife, who accepts the angel's message with awe, Manoah presses for particulars, asking God to reveal through the messenger what the parents are to do for the boy. God listens to his prayer, but interestingly sends the messenger to Manoah's wife, pointedly when she is alone. She includes her husband nevertheless, but he appears foolish in what he says. Unlike his wife, he questions the identity of God's messenger. He appears ignorant of the first message, asking the angel what kind of boy the child will be. The angel simply repeats the first message: His wife knows what to do. She must follow the Nazirite laws. The angel does not have to discuss anything about the boy because the requirements are all in the mother's hands.

Even after the message is given to Manoah, he continues to appear dim-witted. He offers the messenger hospitality; yet the angel replies that a sacrifice to God is in order. The narrator specifies that Manoah still does not recognize God's angel. It is only when the angel ascends in the smoke of the sacrifice that he understands. As a final glimpse into Manoah's misunderstanding, the narrator relates that Manoah believes that he and his wife will die because they have "seen God." There is the view expressed in the Bible that one cannot see the face of God and live, although it is said that Moses viewed God "face to face." In any case, Manoah has seen the *angel* of God, and his wife understands that God would not have accepted their sacrifice and given them these messages—including the birth of the child—if they were to be killed.

The account ends with the fulfillment of the promise. Samson is born, and the spirit of the Lord moves him, as it has moved other judges. Samson's life, however, is troubled. Like his mother of faith, whom the LORD's messenger visited, Samson is consecrated. But like his father, Samson shows poor judgment. He violates the terms of his vow, foolishly allowing himself to be betrayed by foreign women, and he is captured by the Philistines, the very people he was to defeat. But in the final act of his life, he prays to God for one last demonstration of strength, and he crushes the Philistines in their own temple where they had gathered to mock him and his God. At the end of his life, Samson finally mirrored his mother's faith.

Retelling the Story

Some mothers-to-be pray for a handsome son, and some pray for a son whose life will be dedicated to God. In my son, Samson, I had both, and believe me it was no blessing. From his birth our son was consecrated to God as a Nazirite; he would drink no wine, eat no unclean food, and never cut his hair. Even as a boy he was strikingly handsome. It is hard to imagine a mother who would not consider herself blessed by God to have such a son. But I am such a mother—cursed by God to have such a son.

Years ago, when I yearned with all my being for a child, I did hear the announcement of Samson's impending birth as a word of blessing. Manoah and I had prayed for so many years that we would become parents, but our prayers seemed as empty as my womb. Then one day I was visited by a messenger of God. At first I was simply startled, since no man had spoken to me for years except my husband. Then when I realized that this was someone sent from God, I was so frightened I could hardly breathe. The messenger told me I would have a child, a son, and he would be consecrated to God. Had I known then what the future held for me, I would have been terrified.

When my husband returned home, I told him what had happened. At first I think he was jealous, at the very least he was upset. Manoah prayed that God would send the messenger back to us. A short time later, my visitor did return, this time to the field where I sat daydreaming about a baby. He repeated God's promise for me and my husband, telling us how to prepare for the birth and describing the offering we were to make to God in gratitude. At that moment I was so grateful I would have done almost anything to show my appreciation.

When Manoah asks for the name of God's messenger, the angel refuses to answer, saying that "It is a name of wonder" (Judg. 13:18). The rabbis say that there might have been two reasons for the messenger's secrecy. The first was that Samson's parents would never see the angel again and thus didn't need to know his name. The other was that God named each messenger according to the specific mission that angel was on at the time. (*Numbers Rabbah* 10.5)

Samson was a beautiful baby and grew into a strong and handsome boy. He was strong-willed, as well, when it came to something he wanted and was sometimes given to tantrums. Manoah and I passed these behaviors off as the natural result of being an only child. Perhaps, in retrospect, we did indulge him too much. But he was such a beauti-

98

ful child, his uncut hair rippling down his back like water down a waterfall. And he was a gift from God and consecrated to God's service.

As a young man he could have asked to marry any of the young women of Israel, and the only person happier at the match than the father would have been the daughter. But Samson seemed to have no interest in the young women of Israel. He would rather chase after Philistine women, and encourage them to chase after him. Perhaps it was the fact that they were supposed to be as inaccessible as strong drink to him that made them so alluring. All I know is that his desire for foreign women turned my blessing into a curse.

How can one who was loved so well as a child love so badly as a man? How could he be so blind that he could not see the Philistines playing him for the fool? He was never more truly blind after his so-called friends gouged his eyes out than before when he could not see their treachery. Samson, Samson, my son, to them you were no more than an animal to grind their grain, but to me you were to be a blessing.

Now he is dead these many years, and my friends tell me I should be proud that my son died a hero. The same strength that took Samson's life killed many of our enemies in the process. I know they speak in a vain attempt to comfort me. Can they fail to even imagine, though, that I might rather have Samson blind, shaven-headed, and disgraced, but alive in his mother's house, than to hear him called hero and know he is resting next to his father in the ground?

So, listeners, be careful of the blessings you ask of God—you just may receive them. *(Michael E. Williams)*

The rabbis suggest that the Nazarite vow never to cut the hair was a means of intentionally looking as unattractive as possible to keep one from vanity and sexual impurity. It seems that even before a hair on his head was touched, Samson was vain about his strength and promiscuous with foreign women. Cutting his hair and the tragedy of his being blinded seemed to finally protect him from vanity and his passion for Philistine women. Breaking the letter of his vow seemed to help him keep the spirit of it. (*Numbers Rabbah* 10.10)

The Silent Concubine

A Levite goes to retrieve his concubine from her father's house, only to allow her to be raped and left for dead. Then he dismembers her.

The Story

In those days when Israel had no king, a Levite residing in the heart of the hill-country of Ephraim had taken himself a concubine from Bethlehem in Judah. In a fit of anger she had left him and gone to her father's house in Bethlehem in Judah. When she had been there four months, her husband set out after her, with his servant and two donkeys, to appeal to her and bring her back. She brought him into the house of her father, who was delighted to see him and made him welcome. Being pressed by his father-in-law, the girl's father, he stayed there three days, and they were regaled with food and drink during their visit.

On the fourth day, they rose early in the morning, and the Levite prepared to leave, but the father said to his son-in-law, 'Have a bite of something to sustain you before you go,' and the two of them sat down and ate and drank together. The girl's father said to the man, 'Why not spend the night and enjoy yourself?' The man, however, rose to go, but his father-in-law urged him to stay, and again he stayed for the night. He rose early in the morning on the fifth day to depart, but the girl's father said, 'Have something to eat first.' So they lingered till late afternoon, eating and drinking together. Then the man stood up to go with his concubine and his servant, but his father-in-law said, 'Look, the day is wearing on towards sunset. Spend the night here and enjoy yourself, and tomorrow rise early and set out for home.' But the man would not stay the night; he set off on his journey.

He reached a point opposite Jebus, that is Jerusalem, with his two laden donkeys and his concubine. Since they were close to Jebus and the day was nearly gone, the servant said to his master, 'Do let us turn into this Jebusite town for the night.' His master replied, 'No, not into a strange town where the people are not Israelites; let us go on to Gibeah. Come, we will go and find some other place, Gibeah or Ramah, to spend the night.' So they went on until sunset overtook them; they were then near Gibeah which belongs to Benjamin. They turned in there to spend the night, and went and sat down in the open square of the town; but nobody took them into his house for the night.

At nightfall an old man was coming home from his work in the fields. He was from the hill-country of Ephraim, though he lived in Gibeah, where the people were Benjamites. When his eye lighted on the traveller in the town

101

square, he asked him where he was going and where he came from. He answered, 'We are travelling from Bethlehem in Judah to the heart of the hill-country of Ephraim. I come from there; I have been to Bethlehem in Judah and I am going home, but nobody has taken me into his house. I have straw and provender for our donkeys, food and wine for myself, the girl, and the young man; we have all we need.' The old man said, 'You are welcome. I shall supply all your wants; you must not spend the night in the open.' He took him inside, where he provided fodder for the donkeys. Then, having bathed their feet, they all ate and drank.

While they were enjoying themselves, some of the most depraved scoundrels in the town surrounded the house, beating the door violently and shouting to the old man whose house it was, 'Bring out the man who has come to your house, for us to have intercourse with him.' The owner of the house went outside to them and said, 'No, my friends, do nothing so wicked. This man is my guest; do not commit this outrage. Here are my daughter, who is a virgin, and the man's concubine; let me bring them out to you. Abuse them and do what you please; but you must not commit such an outrage against this man.' When the men refused to listen to him, the Levite took his concubine and thrust her outside for them. They raped and abused her all night till the morning; only when dawn broke did they let her go. The woman came at daybreak and collapsed at the entrance of the man's house where her husband was, and lay there until it was light.

Her husband rose in the morning and opened the door of the house to be on his way, and there was his concubine lying at the door with her hands on the threshold. He said to her, 'Get up and let us be off'; but there was no answer. So he lifted her on to his donkey and set off for home.

When he arrived there, he picked up a knife, took hold of his concubine, and cut her limb by limb into twelve pieces, which he then sent through the length and breadth of Israel. He told the men he sent with them to say to every Israelite, 'Has the like of this happened or been seen from the time the Israelites came up from Egypt till today? Consider among yourselves and speak your minds.' Everyone who saw them said, 'Since that time no such thing has ever happened or been seen.'

All the Israelites, the whole community from Dan to Beersheba and also from Gilead, left their homes and as one man assembled before the LORD at Mizpah. The leaders of the people and all the tribes of Israel presented themselves in the assembly of God's people, four hundred thousand foot-soldiers armed with swords. That the Israelites had gone up to Mizpah became known to the Benjamites.

The Israelites asked how this wicked crime happened, and the Levite, to whom the murdered woman belonged, answered, 'I and my concubine arrived at Gibeah in Benjamin to spend the night. The townsmen of Gibeah rose against me that night and surrounded the house where I was, intending to kill me; and they raped my concubine so that she died. I took her and cut her in pieces, and sent the pieces through the length and breadth of Israel, because of the abominable outrage they had committed in Israel. It is for you, the whole of Israel, to come to a decision as to what action should be taken.'

Comments on the Story

Alerting the reader to the problems of anarchy that existed in the time of the judges, the narrator introduces this episode with the telling phrase "in those days when Israel had no king" (v. 1). This view reflects the pro-monarchical opinion within Israelite circles, which held that a king was necessary to deal with the internal disorder and external threats that were too difficult for judges to resolve. In this narrative of the Levite and his concubine, the reader encounters painful incidents. Not only is the life of a powerless, innocent woman violently taken, but the prelude for the mass destruction of the people of Benjamin, Jabesh-gilead, and Shiloh occurs.

The main characters of this account, the Levite and the concubine, are separated by their differences in origin and status. He is of a priestly tribe, a man from the north. Because of her anger or because she had turned to harlotry the woman returns to her father's house. The confusion concerning her motive exists because of the ambiguity of the textual witnesses in verse 2. Only after a period of time has elapsed does the Levite come looking for her, perhaps suggesting a lack of concern on his part.

Once at the father's house, hospitality turns sour, giving the reader a glimpse into the future, more menacing corruption of hospitality that will form the climax to this narrative. At first the father's invitations to his son-in-law seem benign, even gracious. For three days the father entertains the Levite. On the fourth, the Levite prepares to go, but the father again convinces him to stay. As verse 6 makes clear, the father offers his food and hospitality to his son-in-law and not to his own daughter. The provisions are strictly for the enjoyment of the men. Day four does not pass without an interruption in the Levite's plans, for again he is convinced to stay. Surprisingly, on the fifth day his plans are delayed once more, and this time with frightful consequences. After lingering with his father-in-law, the Levite insists upon departing even though the day is well spent and will soon become unsafe for traveling. These days have gone by without any attention paid to the woman. The Levite arrived with the intention of speaking to her heart, but instead keeps lavish company with the father only. By his decision to depart at a late hour, it is obvious that he pays no concern to the woman's comfort or safety.

Upon reaching the town of Jebus, the servant of the Levite suggests that they should spend the night in the safety of that town. Ironically, the Levite does not trust the foreigners and wishes to press on to an Israelite town. By the time they reach Gibeah it is past sunset; it is their only opportunity. Although the Levite feared that the foreigners would be inhospitable, it is his fellow Israelites who deny them a place to stay. The described setting, the town square, recalls the description of another act of hospitality turned to threatened abuse in the Hebrew Bible: the account of Lot at Sodom. The parallels continue. This first reminder sets the menacing tone.

Just as the concubine's father's hospitality at first seemed gracious but later posed a threat to the safety of the travelers, so too does the offer of hospitality by the sojourner in Gibeah hold within it a future menace. The sojourner, an old man from the Levite's home area of Ephraim, asks about their predicament. In describing their plight, the Levite's account mentions the woman but emphasizes his concern for himself. First-person singular references are used six times in verses 18 and 19. When the old man extends an invitation, he uses the second-person *singular* references (v. 20), thereby suggesting what is to come. The words "*you* are welcome. I shall supply all *your* wants; *you* must not spend the night in the open" will prove not to include the woman. She will, in fact, not be welcome, her needs will be violently disregarded, and she will spend the night in the open.

As the scene shifts to the inside of the house, the ominous echo of the narrative of Lot in Sodom is repeated. The description of the depraved men of the town surrounding the house and demanding to have intercourse with—more accurately, to rape—the male guest has occurred before. Just as Lot offered his two virgin daughters as substitutes for his townsmen's lusts, here too the old man offers his own virgin daughter and the Levite's concubine as substitutes to the crowd. Like the men of Sodom, the townsmen of Gibeah refuse the offer, and, just as Lot was more concerned with the (male) angels than with his own daughters, so too do both men disregard the women of the household. When the crowd persists, one of the men, either the Levite himself or the old man, thrusts the Levite's concubine out the door (although this translation specifies that the Levite took this action, the Hebrew text is ambiguous because it reads, literally, "the man seized his concubine"). Unlike the Sodom story, this account is much more menacing. There are no angels to rescue this woman. She is raped by the entire crowd. The language in verse 25 reflects the intense violence by stressing the length of the attack. Throughout the abuse the Levite is conspicuously absent. Even if he did not thrust her out, he said nothing to protest the old man's suggestion. Once she was cast out, he did not protect her or even look for her. The rape and violation continued for the entire night; only when day broke did she arrive at the door and collapse.

The next scene begins with the dramatic statement that the Levite slept through the night and rose to continue his journey! Apparently with no intention of finding his concubine, he stumbles upon her as he opens the door. He expresses no concern or surprise upon seeing her condition; rather, he tells her to arise and prepare to leave. The narrator states that she could not respond. The reader does not know whether she is alive or dead. This gap in our knowledge makes the next scene especially horrific.

Upon reaching home, the Levite dismembers the woman and uses her body to rally the other Israelite tribes against the Benjamites, the tribe in which Gibeah is located. Although there is another text in the Hebrew Bible wherein Saul dismembers an ox in order to rally the tribes to war, clearly the Levite's behavior is outrageous, because Israelite tradition insistently calls for respect for the dead and proper burial. The Levite's uncaring attitude continues to be manifest. In describing his plight, he exaggerates in stating that the Gibeahites intended to kill him. He specifies that they murdered the woman, but the reader knows this is uncertain.

As the account concludes, every suggested action escalates. The Levite's call to action leads to the tribes' demand that the Gibeahites hand over the perpetrators. When they refuse, a civil war breaks out between the tribe of Benjamin and the other Israelites. As the war concludes, the Israelites recognize the horror of the crime against their kinsmen, as the tribe is almost destroyed. Instead of reconsidering their pledge that their daughters not marry the remaining men of Benjamin, they destroy the town of Jabesh-gilead (with the excuse that its people did not support the Israelite attack against Benjamin), saving only the virgins to marry the remaining Benjamites. When the numbers of these women prove to be insufficient, they kidnap women from Shiloh who were participating in a dance.

Throughout this narrative, the concubine never speaks, a reflection of her objectification and powerlessness. Abandoned by her husband, abused by the townsmen, murdered, dismembered—it is difficult to imagine a more terrible end to an innocent life. But the cruelty to her becomes madness as the entire country goes on a rampage. The narrator reflects on the political consequences of anarchy, for at the end of the book of Judges it is written, "In those days there was no king in Israel; everyone did what was right in his own eyes" (21:25). There is no justice for this woman and no happy ending to the book. We are thus compelled to reflect upon the horrors that occur when violence, revenge, and disregard for life go unchecked.

Retelling the Story

In many narrative traditions around the world there are stories of violence, murder, and mutilation. Frequently justice is delayed because the victim has no one to tell what happened. Many times in these stories a body part or bone from the deceased will speak to tell the story of the violation, killing and dismemberment and accuse the guilty party.

DUETS

HANDS

Is it any wonder that we
who had been trained
to serve men
to pleasure men
to feed men
to clothe men
could not save one woman when
men pushed her
and raped her
and hacked her
to pieces.

FEET

Concubines in ancient Israel were most often slaves who had been purchased, captured in battle, or given up by their parents in repayment of a debt. While their "husbands" might father children by them, and those children might have legal status within the family, they were still marginal figures. The rabbis tell that a king might have both a wife and a concubine, but he would visit them in different ways. He would visit his wife publicly, but he would sneak to visit his concubine on the sly. Some of the sages say that God treats Israelites like a wife, coming to them publicly, and the nations like a concubine, seeing them only in secret. (*Genesis Rabbah* 52.5; *Leviticus Rabbah* 1.13)

We carried her to her father's house from which we had taken her years before.
You cannot know the road this woman walks.
After walking the foreign soil of the Jebusites
the streets of Gibeah should have felt like home.
You cannot know the road this woman walks.
No door can finally hold evil out
when fear is pushing you across the threshold.
You cannot know the road this woman walks.
Some call it bad luck and some call it fate.
Some call it neglect and some call it hate.
Doesn't matter what you call it because now it's too late.
You cannot know the road this woman walks.

106

ARMS

Grasped by us he pushed her out.
Seized by us they took her away.
Held by us they took their pleasure.
Pulled by us she measured her way
back to the door that should have protected
and lay at the threshold waiting for day.

LEGS

Run!
Her mind said,
Run!
From the Levite's house,
Run!
From the old man's hold,
Run!
From the crowd's wild shouts,
Run!
From the hands that grasped,
Run!
From the leering stares,
Run!
From the crushing weight,
Run!
From the blood and dirt,
Run!
And get nowhere!

BREASTS

The eyes from whose lustful gaze
we should have been hidden
unleashed on us
their appetite for violence.
The hands that should have caressed
us with loving tenderness
mutilated us
in their appetite for revenge.
The mouths of babies we should have fed
wail in their emptiness

Josephus cleans up the character of the Levite somewhat. He portrays the Levite as being from a vulgar family, but also being very much in love with his concubine. Since she did not love him in the same fashion, they quarreled. These quarrels were the reason for her return home to her family. After she had been raped by the townsmen and fell unconscious at the door of the house where the Levite was staying, he came out to comfort her, according to Josephus. The Levite understood that she had not willingly gone along with their assault. Only when he discovers that she is dead does he dismember her to point up the heinousness of the crime of the Benjamites. (Josephus, *Antiquities*, V, 2.8)

crying for us
with appetites never to be satisfied.

SOLO

TONGUE

Like a lamb before its slaughterers
she spoke no word
at least no one remembered
if she had spoken
called for help
cried out in pain
wept at her loss
sighed at her death.
Like slaughterers before their lamb
no one heard
her words
her calling
her cries
her sobs
her sighs
if, indeed,
there were any.
It does not hurt them
they say.
They like it; they want it,
they say.
She didn't say no,
they say.
They all resist, it's more fun that way,
they say.
She should have told me,
they say.
Meanwhile, a woman's blood
cries out from the earth
and the stones in chorus
mourn her unheard screams
her silent death.
(Michael E. Williams)

RUTH 1:1-18; 3:1-5; 4:1-6, 11-18

Ruth and Naomi

*A Moabite woman becomes the great-grandmother of King David
because of her faithfulness to her mother-in-law, Naomi, and the God of
Naomi.*

The Story

Once, in the time of the Judges when there was a famine in the land, a man from Bethlehem in Judah went with his wife and two sons to live in Moabite territory. The man's name was Elimelech, his wife was Naomi, and his sons were Mahlon and Chilion; they were Ephrathites from Bethlehem in Judah. They came to Moab and settled there.

Elimech died, and Naomi was left a widow with her two sons. The sons married Moabite women, one of whom was called Orpah and the other Ruth. They had lived there about ten years when both Mahlon and Chilion died. Then Naomi, bereaved of her two sons as well as of her husband, got ready to return to her own country with her daughters-in-law, because she heard in Moab that the LORD had shown his care for his people by giving them food. Accompanied by her two daughters-in-law she left the place where she had been living, and they took the road leading back to Judah.

Naomi said to her daughters-in-law, 'Go back, both of you, home to your own mothers. May the LORD keep faith with you, as you have kept faith with the dead and with me; and may he grant each of you the security of a

home with a new husband.' And she kissed them goodbye. They wept aloud and said, 'No, we shall return with you to your people.' But Naomi insisted, 'Go back, my daughters. Why should you come with me? Am I likely to bear any more sons to be husbands for you? Go back, my daughters, go; for I am too old to marry again. But if I could say that I had hope of a child, even if I were to be married tonight and were to bear sons, would you, then, wait until they grew up? Would you on their account remain unmarried? No, my daughters! For your sakes I feel bitter that the LORD has inflicted such misfortune on me.' At this they wept still more. Then Orpah kissed her mother-in-law and took her leave, but Ruth clung to her.

'Look,' said Naomi, 'your sister-in-law has gone back to her people and her god. Go, follow her.' Ruth answered, 'Do not urge me to go back and desert you. Where you go, I shall go, and where you stay, I shall stay. Your people will be my people, and your God my God. Where you die, I shall die, and there be buried. I solemnly declare

109

before the LORD that nothing but death will part me from you.' When Naomi saw that Ruth was determined to go with her, she said no more. . . .

One day Naomi, Ruth's mother-in-law, said to her, 'My daughter, I want to see you settled happily. Now there is our kinsman Boaz, whose girls you have been with. Tonight he will be winnowing barley at the threshing-floor. Bathe and anoint yourself with perfumed oil, then get dressed and go down to the thresh-ing-floor; but do not make yourself known to the man until he has finished eating and drinking. When he lies down make sure you know the place where he is. Then go in, turn back the cover-ing at his feet and lie down. He will tell you what to do.' 'I will do everything you say,' replied Ruth. . . .

Boaz meanwhile had gone up to the town gate and was sitting there when the next-of-kin of whom he had spoken came past. Calling him by name, Boaz cried, 'Come over here and sit down.' He went over and sat down. Boaz also stopped ten of the town's elders and asked them to sit there. When they were seated he addressed the next-of-kin: "You will remember the strip of field that belonged to our kinsman Elim-elech. Naomi is selling it, now that she has returned from Moab. I promised to open the matter with you, to ask you to acquire it in the presence of those sit-ting here and in the presence of the elders of my people. If you are going to do your duty as next-of-kin, then do so; but if not, someone must do it. So tell me, and then I shall know, for I come

after you as next-of-kin." He answered "I shall act as next-of-kin." Boaz contin-ued: 'On the day you take over the field from Naomi, I take over the widow, Ruth the Moabite, so to perpetuate the name of the dead man on his holding.' 'Then I cannot act,' said the next-of-kin, 'lest it should be detrimental to my own holding; and as I cannot act, you your-self must take over my duty as next-of-kin.' . . . All who were at the gate, including the elders, replied, 'We are witnesses. May the LORD make this woman, who is about to come into your home, to be like Rachel and Leah, the two who built up the family of Israel. May you do a worthy deed in Ephrathah by keeping this name alive in Bethle-hem. Through the offspring the LORD gives you by this young woman may your family be like the family of Perez, whom Tamar bore to Judah.'

So Boaz took Ruth and she became his wife. When they had come together the LORD caused her to conceive, and she gave birth to a son. The women said to Naomi, 'Blessed be the LORD, who has not left you this day without next-of-kin. May the name of your dead son be kept alive in Israel! The child will give you renewed life and be your support and stay in your old age, for your devoted daughter-in-law, who has proved better to you than seven sons, has borne him.' Naomi took the child and laid him in her own lap, and she became his foster-mother. Her women neighbors gave him a name: 'Naomi has a son; we shall call him Obed,' they said. He became the father of Jesse, David's father.

Comments on the Story

Ruth is one of only two books of the Hebrew Bible that bear a woman's name, and there is debate whether the book of Ruth serves as a model of women's faithfulness and the acceptance of foreigners, or as a tract that is wary of Gentiles and is insistent upon keeping control over independent women.

The book opens with surprising information. In the presence of famine, Elimelech flees with his family to Moab. In the Hebrew Bible, Moab is known as a place of sexual licentiousness, apostasy, and idolatry; indeed, Elimelech and his family will only find suffering and death there. Elimelech and his two sons, Mahlon and Chilion, die, and the sons' Moabite wives have been infertile. The three widows, without means and normally without a voice for their own future, take initiative. Hearing that God has once again provided food in her own country, the widowed Naomi sets out to return to Judah accompanied by her daughters-in-law, Orpah and Ruth, until Naomi challenges them to return to their own land. Naomi recognizes the faith and loyalty they have shown her, but insists they return to their own people so they can have the security of husbands and escape the hardships of widowhood. Just as Naomi sees that her daughters-in-law have little value if they remain widowed, she also expresses her own worth in terms of her ability to bear children. She laments that she is too old. She frames her inability in terms that recall the levirate marriage—the custom of the dead man's brother or next of kin marrying the widow so that the deceased's name and progeny will continue and the inheritance will not be lost outside the family. This scene anticipates the discussion that Boaz and the unnamed kinsman will have concerning who will marry Ruth.

Ruth's insistence that she stay with Naomi is striking. Making no reference to her uncertain future as a widow, she says that she will stay by Naomi's side, accepting her people and her God, continuing her loyalty until death. Although some interpreters point to Naomi's lack of response to Ruth and to her comments to the townspeople that she has returned empty to be an implicit rejection of Naomi's worth, it is also possible that she is so filled with her own grief that even Ruth's loyalty to her cannot erase her feelings of overwhelming loss.

After Ruth has had the good fortune to meet Boaz while gleaning in the fields, Naomi reveals that he is actually their kinsman and hopes that he will marry Ruth. Although for some interpreters Naomi's previous silence concerning the existence of such a kinsman is an indication of her lack of concern for Ruth, it may reveal a custom whereby a woman was powerless to take the initiative to have the widow provided for by a man (the Tamar story of Genesis 38 may also be indicative of this phenomenon). Like Rebekah, who took the initiative and devised a successful plan to secure the blessing for Jacob, Naomi describes a plan to have Ruth win the heart of Boaz and thus find security. Ruth is to enhance her beauty, meet him at the threshing floor (associated with sexual activity in other places in the Bible), and secretly approach him after he has eaten and drunk and is lying down. The most arresting item of her speech is Naomi's advice for Ruth to "turn back the covering at his feet" (3:4). "To uncover the feet" may be used as a euphemism meaning to have sexual relations. Although the text does not make clear whether Ruth and Boaz have relations, the possibility is not excluded, and indeed the ambiguity continues when Boaz is concerned that Ruth depart when no one can see her.

Although Naomi predicted that Boaz would take the directive when his feet were uncovered, it was Ruth who acts with initiative, requests Boaz's protection, and implicitly asks for marriage. Boaz complies by recognizing her loyalty to her mother-in-law and to Israel, but insists on checking with the unnamed kinsman who is first in line to redeem Mahlon's property (land and wife!). The translation of 4:5 is problematic. Some biblical translations have "I [Boaz] take over the widow, Ruth the Moabite," whereas other tranlations have "you [the kinsman]. . . . " If the reference to Boaz is correct, then the kinsman rejects buying the property because he feels his rights to it will be threatened by a future heir that may be born to Ruth and Boaz. If the reference is to the requirement that the kinsman must also marry Ruth if he wants the property, then the kinsman is refusing the land because he wants no part of Ruth. In either case, Boaz's fidelity to Ruth and recognition of her virtue contrast with the kinsman who rejects her and his responsibility to Israelite law. Boaz proclaims his intentions publicly, the townspeople express their hopes for Ruth's fertility, and in a telling remark, they hope that her offspring will be like the line of Judah and Tamar. The comparison of Ruth with Tamar is appropriate. Both women were widows and came close to remaining without additional husbands and offspring, even though there were men who were designated as responsible kinsmen. Both women found the progenitors of their children because of their own initiative. Both women prompt the reconsideration of stereotypes: Tamar because she was unfairly associated with the deaths of her husband and brother-in-law and because she posed as a prostitute but was judged righteous; and Ruth because she was a Moabite who became a loyal member of the Israelite community.

Once Ruth bears a child, the reader no longer learns of her perspective. Naomi receives the attention from the women of the town, who name the boy Obed, and Naomi cares for the child. Could it be that the narrator remains uncomfortable with a Moabitess as a role model and thus wishes to stress Obed's Israelite ancestry through Naomi? Or perhaps having already made the point that Ruth is Obed's mother, the narrator is bringing the account of Naomi's tragedy full circle. The woman who was so distraught that she changed her name to Mara ("bitter") is now joyful. Although the end of the book shifts its focus away from Ruth, it is still clear that she and the other woman recalled, Tamar, are righteous women, important in their own right and as the ancestresses of King David. Some commentators have pointed out an additional purpose that is served by this book. It provides an alternative perspective to the books of Ezra and Nehemiah, which so fear the intermarriage of Israelites with foreigners. In this book, the foreigner Ruth serves as a model of loyalty to the Israelite community.

The story of Ruth shows us the pervasiveness of patriarchal structures. Women have no place to turn when they are widowed and fear for their very survival. Both women and men see women's worth in terms of whether they can bear sons. Ruth was willing to challenge some of society's expectations of her—she left her homeland and went to a land where she would be suspect. Her legacy in Israel was celebrated in patriarchal terms—she is praised for being the mother of King David—but Ruth's words of comfort and loyalty to Naomi point to a more timeless theme.

Retelling the Story

The exiles were returning from captivity, and Ezra and Nehemiah wanted to create a pure faith. It is little wonder, since they had seen the people of God turn to idol worship in the land of their captivity. So they told the people to put away those foreign husbands and foreign wives, put away those children who could not even speak or read the holy language. In the midst of their purifying of the tribe, a storyteller whose name is now forgotten remembered this story:

In the time when the judges ruled, when people did whatever seemed right in their own eyes, there was a man named Elimelech and his wife, Naomi, from Bethlehem in Judah. There was a famine across that part of the country, and this couple left their homeland to move to Moab. Why they would choose to live among a God-forsaken people no one knows. Perhaps the crops were good there.

In any case, the two sons of Elimelech and Naomi, Mahlon and Chilion, married two Moabite women, one named Orpah and the other Ruth. Why they didn't send their sons back home to wed good Jewish girls from nice families no one can figure. A short time later, though, the worst tragedy that could befall a woman came to Naomi. Her husband, Elimelech, died. Then the worst tragedy beyond the worst tragedy happened: Her two sons died.

So there was Naomi, in a foreign country with no husband or sons. Instead she was stuck with two *Moabite* daughters-in-law. So she did the only reasonable thing: She packed to return to her home, Bethlehem. Also she tried to talk her two Moabite daughters-in-law into staying in their home country. She told them, "I am returning to *my* people." But they refused. Perhaps they did not know what Naomi did, that they would never be accepted among her people. The Torah said clearly that, while Egyptians and Edomites could become a part of the community in three generations, no *Moabite* could enter the household of faith even after ten generations.

> The sages say that Ruth's speech to Naomi reflected a conversation and that certain parts of it were offered in answer to specific statements by Naomi. Naomi's part of the conversation unfortunately was not included in the Scripture text. For example, when Ruth said she would go with Naomi, her mother-in-law, responded that Jewish women did not go to theaters and circuses. To this Ruth responded that she would simply follow Naomi's example, "Wherever you go I will go." Then Naomi told her that she could not live in a house that did not have a mezuzah on the door. Ruth replied, "Wherever you live I will live." When Ruth said, "Your people will be my people," she was saying, "I will leave all idolatry behind." And with, "Your God will be my God," Ruth expressed her dependence on the God of Israel alone. (*Ruth Rabbah* 2.22-23)

So she tried again to dissuade them. "At my age, will I give birth to sons whom you could marry and with whom you could have children? Even if I could, would you wait for them to grow to manhood before starting your families? No, you must marry one of your own kind." Orpah saw the wisdom in Naomi's words, kissed her mother-in-law, and returned to her home. But Ruth refused. "Don't you tell me to leave you and stop following after you. Wherever you go, I am going; and wherever you stay, I'll stay. Your people will be my people and your God my God. Wherever you die, I'll die, and they can bury me next to you. Only death will separate you from me."

> The rabbis say that the day Naomi and Ruth entered Bethlehem was the day that the whole town turned out to mourn with Boaz the death of his wife. When they saw Naomi, they were shocked by her appearance. Before she had been carried everywhere by servants; now she was barefoot. Before she had worn clothes of the finest wool; now she was dressed in tattered rages. Before her face had been full and full of color from good food and drink; now she was pale, and her cheeks were hollow from hunger. After they saw her in such a state, it made sense to them when she said, "Don't call me Naomi ['pleasant']. Rather call me Mara ['bitter']." (*Ruth Rabbah* 3.6)

Great! Naomi was stuck for life *with a Moabite daughter-in-law*. In time they returned to Bethlehem—and Naomi's kinsfolk greeted her with, "Naomi, welcome . . . who in the world is that Moabite woman dragging after you?"— Naomi answered her, "Don't call me Naomi. Call me Mara ["bitter"], for my life has been a bitter one; my husband and sons are dead, and now I have a Moabite daughter-in-law. God has dealt bitterly with me." They would all sympathize.

Upon their return to Bethlehem, Naomi and Ruth began to take part in the Israelite welfare system called gleaning. Farmers were forbidden to go back over a harvested field to gather what grain had fallen. Rather, what fell in the field was to be gathered, or "gleaned," by the poor. Gleaning could be a dangerous business, as is often true for the lives of the poor, especially women, since there were those who would hit them in the head, or worse, to get what they wanted.

It just so happened, though, that Ruth went to glean in a field owned by Boaz, a kinsman of Naomi's late husband. When he noticed the foreign woman gleaning in his fields, Boaz asked who she was and was told of her relationship with Naomi and how hard she had worked during the day. He went to her and told her to drink from his workers' jars of water and to glean in no fields but his, and she would be protected. When Ruth asked why he would show such kindness to a foreigner, he told her he had heard of her kindness toward his kinswoman Naomi. "May the God of Israel, under whose wings you have taken refuge, bless you." Then he asked her to eat her meal with him and his people, and he instructed his workers to drop extra grain for her to pick up.

The thing that first attracted Boaz to Ruth, according to the sages, was her modesty. While the other women who gleaned bent over and hitched up their skirts to pick up grain, Ruth left her skirt down and knelt to gather hers. While the other women joked and flirted with the hired hands, Ruth kept to herself. While the other gleaners went between the sheaves to gather their grain, Ruth waited until the sheaves were brought in and gathered only after everything but the gleanings had been taken out of the field. (*Ruth Rabbah* 4.6)

When Ruth returned home that night she told Naomi, "I met the nicest man today, a kinsman of yours named Boaz. I think he took a liking to me." Suddenly the wheels in Naomi's mind started turning. She said, "When the barley harvest is over, go to see Boaz by night on the threshing floor. Put on your prettiest dress and your most alluring perfume. When you arrive he will be sleeping, so *uncover his feet,*" at these words she gave Ruth a knowing wink, "and then do whatever he tells you when he wakes up." Now, this does not sound like very good advice on the face of it, but Naomi must have known what she was doing.

When the harvest was done, Ruth did just what her mother-in-law had instructed. She went to the threshing floor and *uncovered Boaz's feet.* When he awoke, Boaz told her, "What a wise young woman you are. You didn't run after one of these young men. Rather, you came to a man who had a little gray in his beard. Leave while it is still dark, taking this basket of barley with you, and leave the rest to me." So she did.

Many of the sages were very clear that nothing inappropriate went on between Ruth and Boaz on the threshing floor. But that doesn't mean that he wasn't tempted. The Evil Inclination said to Boaz, "Look, you're single. She's single. Just make her your wife here and now by having sex with her. Who will know?" But Boaz said, "As God lives I will not lay a finger on her." And he kept his promise until after they were wed. (*Ruth Rabbah* 4.4)

The next day, Boaz went to the city gate where the men gathered to discuss important matters of the day and approached a closer kinsman to Naomi's late husband. Boaz asked him, "Since Naomi has come home, somebody needs to do something about that piece of property that belonged to Elimelech. Are you interested? You're the first in line to say so, if you are." The man replied, "Well, you know I could do with a few more fields of barley." Then Boaz added, as if it were of no real importance, "You know, if you take the property you have to take the Moabite woman who came home with Naomi."

"In that case," the man retorted, "I'll let it pass to you, if you're crazy enough to take it. To take a Moabite into your household would ruin your family line."

"Fine," was Boaz's only reply. He married Ruth, and before long they had a son they named Obed. All the women came to Naomi and told her, "You have a daughter-in-law who is better than seven sons." In the terms of that time, this meant they thought she was better than just about anything anybody could imagine.

How could a Moabite woman become the great-grandmother of King David? After all, Deuteronomy says that no Moabite can become a member of the community for ten generations. Ah, the rabbis say, the Torah doesn't say that a Moabitess could not be welcomed. (*Ruth Rabbah* 4.1)

And just in case Ezra and Nehemiah and the purification party didn't get it, the storyteller added that Obed was the father of Jesse, who was the father of David, the king. All from the line of a Moabite woman. (*Michael E. Williams*)

Hannah

Hannah prays for a son, and her prayer is answered in Samuel. The problem is that she had promised the son back to God's service and has to give him up.

The Story

There was a certain man from Ramathaim, a Zuphite from the hill-country of Ephraim, named Elkanah son of Jeroham, son of Elihu, son of Tohu, son of Zuph and Ephraimite. He had two wives, Hannah and Peninnah; Peninnah had children, but Hannah was childless. Every year this man went up from his town to worship and offer sacrifice to the LORD of Hosts at Shiloh, where Eli's two sons, Hophni and Phinehas, were priests of the LORD.

When Elkanah sacrificed, he gave several shares of the meat to his wife Peninnah with all her sons and daughters; but to Hannah he gave only one share; the LORD had not granted her children, yet it was Hannah whom Elkanah loved. Hannah's rival also used to torment and humiliate her because she had no children. This happened year after year when they went up to the house of the LORD: her rival used to torment her, until she was in tears and would not eat. Her husband Elkanah said to her, 'Hannah, why are you crying and eating nothing? Why are you so miserable? Am I not more to you than ten sons?'

After they had finished eating and drinking at the sacrifice at Shiloh, Hannah rose in deep distress, and weeping bitterly stood before the LORD and prayed to him. Meanwhile Eli the priest was sitting on his seat beside the door of the temple of the LORD. Hannah made this vow. "LORD of Hosts, if you will only take notice of my trouble and remember me, if you will not forget me but grant me offspring, then I shall give the child to the LORD for the whole of his life, and no razor shall ever touch his head.'"

For a long time she went on praying before the LORD, while Eli watched her lips. Hannah was praying silently; her lips were moving although her voice could not be heard, and Eli took her for a drunken woman. 'Enough of this drunken behaviour!' he said to her. 'Leave off until the effect of the wine has gone.' 'Oh, sir!' she answered, 'I am a heart-broken woman; I have drunk neither wine nor strong drink, but I have been pouring out my feelings before the LORD. Do not think me so devoid of shame, sir; all this time I have been speaking out of the depths of my grief and misery.' Eli said, 'Go in peace, and may the God of Israel grant what you have asked of him.' Hannah replied, 'May I be worthy of your kindness.' And no longer downcast she went away and had something to eat.

Next morning they were up early and, after prostrating themselves before the LORD, returned to their home

117

at Ramah. Elkanah had intercourse with his wife Hannah, and the LORD remembered her; she conceived, and in due time bore a son, whom she named Samuel, 'because,' she said, 'I asked the LORD for him.'

Elkanah with his whole household went up to make the annual sacrifice to the LORD and to keep his vow. Hannah did not go; she said to her husband, 'After the child is weaned I shall come up with him to present him before the LORD: then he is to stay there always.' Her husband Elkanah said to her, 'Do what you think best; stay at home until you have weaned him. Only, may the LORD indeed see your vow fulfilled.' So the woman stayed behind and nursed her son until she had weaned him.

When she had weaned him, she took him up with her. She took also a bull three years old, an ephah of flour, and a skin of wine, and she brought him, child as he was, into the house of the LORD at Shiloh. When the bull had been slaughtered, Hannah brought the boy to Eli and said, 'Sir, as sure as you live, I am the woman who stood here beside you praying to the LORD. It was this boy that I prayed for and the LORD has granted what I asked. Now I make him over to the LORD; for his whole life he is lent to the LORD.' And they prostrated themselves there before the LORD.

Comments on the Story

The books of Samuel consist of reflections on the transition period in Israel from rule by the judges to rule by the kings. The central authority of the king would facilitate the definitive victory over the Philistines, but would also be problematic because of abuse of power. It is within this setting that Hannah gives birth to Samuel, the anointer of Israel's first kings. Like the matriarchs who suffer from infertility, Hannah endures the anguish of her inability to have children. Yet God responds to her prayer.

As the account opens, the depth of Hannah's suffering is apparent. She is not the only wife of Elkanah; she shares her husband with Peninnah and "all her [Peninnah's] sons and daughters" (v. 4). The narrator shows that in spite of Hannah's misfortune, Elkanah loves her and not Peninnah. Nonetheless, childlessness causes the unrelieved ache in Hannah's heart, and love from her husband cannot eliminate it. Peninnah is cruel to Hannah, tormenting and humiliating her on days of sacrifice, pointing to the low status of a childless woman. When Elkanah appeals to Hannah to give up her depression he seems to express his love for her: "Am I not more to you than ten sons?" It must be noted, however, that he *does* have children through Peninnah, whereas Hannah has none by any man. Although the narrator states that it is Hannah whom Elkanah loves, some commentators suggest that his statement about her childlessness shows a lack of sensitivity.

Whatever his feelings for her, Hannah stands alone when she faces the pain of childlessness, so she appeals to the Lord. Her prayer is proleptic of

God's response to her. She addresses God with the title "LORD of Hosts," usually used to refer to the God who fights for Israel against oppression. In addition, she promises that if she has an offspring, the child will be dedicated as a Nazirite for life. When her child Samuel is born, Israel is at the threshold of tremendous political change in its governing system. The vow for the child to be a Nazirite is reminiscent of Samson's birth and the days of the judges, but Samuel marks the passage into the days of the kings, when Israel will have rest from the oppression of the Philistines. Hannah's vow that the child will be a Nazirite until his death is striking. When the description of the rules of the Nazirite are given in Numbers 6, it is presumed that the time of service is limited. Hannah promises that her child's service will be unusual.

Hannah's pledge is significant for another reason. By promising life-long servitude, Hannah denies herself the comfort of being near her child. Although her motive is not stated, one commentator suggests that she considers the first child an offering to enable her to have additional children. In any case, the narrator indicates that God rewards her for her dedication, and she has five other children (2:21).

Just as Elkanah does not understand the depth of her pain, so too does the priest at Shiloh misconstrue her prayer. The narrator states that she "rose in deep distress, and weeping bitterly stood before the LORD and prayed to him . . . for a long time she went on praying before the LORD" (vv. 9, 12). In spite of this moving scene, Eli remonstrates her, calling her a drunkard because he had seen her lips move but could not hear her voice. Hannah defends herself. When Eli responds kindly and prays that the Lord hear her prayer, she has hope.

God responds; Hannah has a son and names him Samuel, which in popular etymology could be understood to mean "he who is from God," recalling her words "I asked the LORD for him" (v. 20). Commentators have pointed out that her expression would correspond more directly to the name "Saul," which comes from the same root as the word for "ask." This and other references persuade many that elements of an original birth story about Saul have been combined with Samuel's.

It is interesting to note that the birth of Samuel was a gift from God in response to Hannah's prayer and insistence and that Elkanah never prayed to God on behalf of his wife. Elkanah does not even perceive the need for another child because he has others with Penninah. Thus it is appropriate that without consulting Elkanah, Hannah names the child. Once her son is born, Hannah decides to remain with him while the others go to sacrifice, knowing that she will be faithful to the Nazirite vow when the time comes for her son to be dedicated. Like that of many women in the Bible, Hannah's story is included because she is the mother of an important man. Yet her faith and initiative in spite of suffering and misunderstanding prompted God's action and led to the birth of the one who would help Israel in a troubled time.

Retelling the Story

There is a woman named Hannah, much loved by her husband, Elkanah. But she has no children.

Elkanah has another wife, Penninah. Hannah is his favorite, but Penninah has borne him children.

Each year Elkanah travels with his family from Ramah to Shiloh, to celebrate with sacrifice and feasting. At the feasting when he distributes the food, he gives to Hannah one portion—for herself. To Penninah he gives many portions. Of course, she has many children to feed.

Penninah—who is jealous of Hannah because Elkanah loves her more—cannot resist this chance to shame her rival. She taunts, looking at the disparate piles of food. "See, it's because you have no children. I have many children. What kind of wife are you?"

Year after year it goes on this way. Hannah becomes more and more desperate with her own sadness, more and more irritated at Penninah's goading her, rubbing it in about her childlessness.

One year it gets so bad that Hannah weeps and refuses to eat.

Her husband tries to comfort her. "You know I love you. How can you be sad, knowing how much I love you? Am I not worth more than ten sons?"

Hannah looks at him aghast. What is he talking about? Doesn't he know it's a different issue completely? Of course, she's happy to have his love, but in no way does that make up for the lack of children.

She stumbles to her feet and leaves the table. Still weeping, she hurries out into a courtyard and sinks down on the steps of the temple. Her lips move in a prayer, though she makes no sound. She prays, "O Lord, have mercy on me in my misery. Give me a son. If you will give me a son, he will be yours all the days of his life."

A priest of the temple, Eli, happens to be sitting nearby and, seeing Hannah's lips moving in such agitation but hearing no sound, he assumes she is drunk.

"Dear lady," he says, take it easy with the wine. It's going to take a while for even this much to wear off."

"Oh, you're wrong," she says. "I'm not drunk. I'm terribly upset. I've been praying to the Lord out of sorrow and frustration."

"Well," says the priest, "in that case go in peace, and may God grant you your wish."

She feels a lot better then, and she goes home to Ramah with her husband and family. Sure enough, the Lord grants her wish. She conceives and bears a son. She remembers her promise, and she names the child Samuel.

> The traditional day that God remembered Hannah and she conceived was the first day of the new year, Rosh Hoshanna. The same was suggested for Sarah and Rachel, that they conceived on the new year. This was the day God remembered the people and did favors for them. (*Genesis Rabbah* 73.1)

But when it is time for Elkanah to take his family to the reunion feast again, she demurs. "Not yet," she says, looking longingly at her son. "I am still nursing him. I can't give him up yet."

"All right," Elkanah says. "But remember your vow." And he goes to the feast without her.

This time when Penninah receives her portions of food, there is no Hannah for her to torment. Hannah is home, enjoying her son. She could care less about missing the feast.

The time came around again, and again, and then once more it is time to go for the reunion feast. Hannah knows she can put off no longer her compliance with her vow to give her son to the Lord.

She and Elkanah gather gifts for the temple and for Eli, the priest, and they take Samuel with them and go to Shiloh, where the temple is.

They take the child Samuel to Eli. "Remember me?" Hannah says. "I'm the one who was so distraught that you thought I was drunk. I had promised that if I had a son he would be the Lord's. You blessed me. When I left I was calmed and at peace. I did conceive, and I have come to make good on my vow—to lend my child to the Lord for all his life."

Eli smiles at her. "Lend?" he says. "If it is for all his life, is it not a gift out-right?"

> The rabbis seem to have a profound respect for the power of Hannah's prayer. In several places they say that Korah and his followers, who had rebelled against Moses, were punished by descending deeper and deeper into a pit. The only thing that stopped his descent was Hannah's saying that God "sends down to Sheol" and "brings the dead up again" (1 Sam. 2:6). Only the words of this pious woman could stop Korah's free fall into the void. (*Genesis Rabbah* 98.2)

But Hannah clings to Samuel a moment longer. "Perhaps," she says. "But my heart is heavy to be parting from him. I shall come again each year to see him. If it makes me feel better to think of it as a loan, what is that to you?"

And Eli is silent, for he recognizes that while she is glad to give her son to the Lord, there is pain in the woman's heart as well. *(Martha Whitmore Hickman)*

Bathsheba

Taken by King David as his lover, then wife, Bathsheba experiences the death of her husband Uriah and her child and finally sees her son Solomon succeed his father to the throne.

The Story

At the turn of the year, when kings go out to battle, David sent Joab out with his other officers and all the Israelite forces, and they ravaged Ammon and laid siege to Rabbah.

David remained in Jerusalem, and one evening, as he got up from his couch and walked about on the roof of the palace, he saw from there a woman bathing, and she was very beautiful. He made enquiries about the woman and was told, 'It must be Bathsheba daughter of Eliam and wife of Uriah the Hittite.' He sent messengers to fetch her, and when she came to him, he had intercourse with her, though she was still purifying herself after her period, and then she went home. She conceived, and sent word to David that she was pregnant.

David ordered Joab to send Uriah the Hittite to him. Joab did so, and when Uriah arrived, David asked him for news of Joab and the troops and how the campaign was going, and then said to him, 'Go down to your house and wash your feet after your journey.' As he left the palace, a present from the king followed him. Uriah, however, did not return to his house; he lay down by the palace gate with all the king's ser-

vants. David, learning that Uriah had not gone home, said to him, 'You have had a long journey; why did you not go home?' Uriah answered, 'Israel and Judah are under canvas, and so is the Ark, and my lord Joab and your majesty's officers are camping in the open; how can I go home to eat and drink and to sleep with my wife? By your life, I cannot do this!' David then said to Uriah, 'Stay here another day, and tomorrow I shall let you go.' So Uriah stayed in Jerusalem that day. On the following day David invited him to eat and drink with him and made him drunk. But in the evening Uriah went out to lie down in his blanket among the king's servants and did not go home.

In the morning David wrote a letter to Joab and sent it with Uriah. In it he wrote, 'Put Uriah opposite the enemy where the fighting is fiercest and then fall back, and leave him to meet his death.' So Joab, during the siege of the city, stationed Uriah at the point where he knew the enemy had expert troops. The men of the city sallied out and engaged Joab, and some of David's guards fell; Uriah the Hittite was also killed. Joab sent David a dispatch with all the news of the battle and gave the messenger these instructions: 'When you have finished your report to the king, he may be angry and ask, "Why did you go so near the city during the fight? You must have known there would be shooting from the wall. Remember who killed Abimelech son of Jerubbesheth. Was it not a woman who threw down an upper millstone on him from the wall of Thebez and killed him? Why did you go near the wall?"—if he asks this, then tell him, "Your servant Uriah the Hittite also is dead.". . .

When Uriah's wife heard that her husband was dead, she mourned for him. . . .

. . . Nathan said to David, 'You are the man! This is the word of the LORD the God of Israel to you: I anointed you king over Israel, I gave you your master's daughter and his wives to be your own, I gave you the daughters of Israel and Judah; and, had this not been enough, I would have added other favours as well. Why then have you flouted the LORD's word by doing what is wrong in my eyes? You have struck down Uriah the Hittite with the sword; the man himself you murdered by the sword of the Ammonites, and you have stolen his wife. Now, therefore, since you have despised me and taken the wife of Uriah the Hittite to be your own wife, your family will never again have rest from the sword. This is the word of the LORD: I shall bring trouble on you from within your own family. I shall take your wives and give them to another man before your eyes, and he will lie with them in broad daylight. What you did was done in secret; but I shall do this in broad daylight for all Israel to see." David said to Nathan, 'I have sinned against the LORD.' Nathan answered, 'The LORD has laid on another the consequences of your sin: you will not die, but, since by this deed you have shown your contempt for the LORD, the child who will be born to you shall die.'. . .

. . . David consoled Bathsheba his wife; he went to her and had intercourse with her, and she gave birth to a son and called him Solomon. And because the LORD loved him, he sent word through Nathan the prophet that for the LORD's sake he would be given the name Jedidiah.

Comments on the Story

The story of Bathsheba is part of the narrative about the family intrigues of King David. It reveals the weaknesses of David and other members of his family that lead to rivalry for the throne, violence, and death. The account of Bathsheba and David tells of David's sins, God's judgment, and the birth of Solomon, the son of David and Bathsheba, who succeeds David to the throne. It also reveals the powerlessness of a woman who suffers because of the acts of royalty.

The scene opens at a time of year "when kings go out to battle," but King David has sent his officers to fight battles while he remains at home. Because the reason is not given for his lack of involvement in crucial battles, the reader is allowed to speculate. Is David shirking his duty as commander-in-chief? Does he lack courage? Is he old or weak? When he sees Bathsheba, he is resting on his couch, hardly the image of a warrior.

Seeing the beautiful Bathsheba bathing from a roof top, David asks who she is. Hearing that she is another man's wife does not stop him from sending for her and having intercourse with her. The reference to her bathing has set the stage for crucial information: Bathsheba was purifying herself from her menstrual periods, a religious custom done before resuming intercourse. This detail about her menstrual cycle enables the reader to be certain that she is not already pregnant by her husband when she has intercourse with David. Is Bathsheba at all responsible for the adulterous relationship? The narrator provides no direct evidence that she is. Although this gap allows for the possibility that she chose to bathe in the view of the king, the alternative and more likely possibility is that she is merely following the pious tradition of taking the ritual bath in her own vicinity. She did not initiate contact with the king; indeed, we can presume that she could not even see him without being sent for. Once she is there, there is no description of what occurred. Although some assume that she seduced him, one could speculate more safely that he raped her, given that David initiated the meeting. How could a lone woman stop a king?

After the affair has occurred, we learn of the location of Bathsheba's husband. While David was enjoying an adulterous affair, Uriah was fighting the king's battles! Thus, when Bathsheba sends word to David that she is pregnant, she can be certain that he is the father. David's injustices continue. With the hopes of completing a plan wherein he could trick Uriah into thinking that he is the father of the child, David sends for Uriah and proceeds to inquire about the war. But the king's true motivation for calling Uriah home becomes clear when he states, "Go down to your house and wash your feet after your journey" (v. 8). The words are appropriate given that washing one's feet may be a euphemism for sexual relations. Uriah leaves the king's presence; David assumes his plan will work and that Uriah will sleep with his wife, thus concealing David's paternity. Unexpectedly, Uriah sleeps among the palace servants. When David inquires why, Uriah stresses his faithfulness as a soldier. His refusal to partake in the comforts of home contrast with David's refusal to be with his troops. David insists that Uriah stay another day, using the veil of hospitality to make Uriah drunk, thus weakening his resolve. Still, Uriah refuses to go home.

Having failed to cover his fatherhood of Bathsheba's expectant child, David decides to have Uriah killed. Returning to the front, the innocent Uriah bears the message precipitating his own death. He brings a letter from David to Joab, the commander, which directs Joab to place Uriah in the most dangerous combat position, thereby ensuring his death. Joab complies with the order, but in so doing also loses other elite soldiers. Joab knows David will be angry when he hears of the other deaths and instructs the messenger to David to withhold the information about Uriah's death until David learns of the deaths of his guards.

Joab proves prescient. After David expresses his rage over their deaths, he quickly relents upon hearing that Uriah is dead too. He then sends words of comfort to Joab, stating that unintended tragedies occur in battle. Such an opportunistic change of heart makes David's plot to kill Uriah appear more malign. Because Uriah is dead, David callously overlooks the innocent deaths of others. David's lust turned to adultery, the adultery necessitated concealing paternity, the deceit led to one murder, and the execution of the plan led to the deaths of others. The death of Uriah makes Bathsheba a widow whose unborn child is destined to be an orphan. The reader never learns of the silent Bathsheba's perspective, an indication of her powerlessness.

David married Bathsheba after her period of mourning was over. His motive is not stated, but perhaps he wants to preempt her from revealing the father of her child. At the end of verse 27, the narrator finally gives God's perspective: David's actions were wrong. By waiting until this point, all of David's actions can be included in the condemnation.

Although David is king, his sin does not go unchecked. The prophet Nathan reveals God's judgment to David. Nathan confirms what the reader would ask—is this how David repays the LORD for all God has given him? The judgment is harsh: The child Bathsheba is carrying will die. The sad tale has one more death, and again Bathsheba is the innocent victim. Widowed because of David's sin, she is now bereft of her child. The final verses of this pericope finally show some tenderness on David's part. He consoles Bathsheba for the death of their son. They have another child, Solomon—the one who will succeed David to the throne, who will be known for his wisdom, and who will build the Temple in Jerusalem.

This tragic tale does not reveal Bathsheba's perspective while she is being used by the most powerful man in Israel. Although she is neglected, the reader can see how wrong it is that the innocent suffer when the powerful assert their prerogatives. But in Israel, the sins of even the king will not go unanswered. Most difficult to accept is that as David's sin is punished, Bathsheba must endure the death of her small son. Israel learns the painful lesson that as individual sin is punished, the innocent may bear the burden.

Retelling the Story

One spring afternoon, having finished my household chores (which were at a minimum with my husband, Uriah, off fighting the Ammonites) I was bathing in my walled courtyard when in through the gate stomped two men, wearing some kind of court uniform.

"Who are you?" I asked, quickly covering myself. "What are you doing here?"

"Messengers of the king," they said. "Come, King David wants to see you."

126

"For what?" I asked. The king, who is virtually our neighbor, is known to have a wandering eye for women.

"Just come along," they said. And they picked me up and carried me off to the palace.

There, among all that purple hanging, all that gold, was the king! King David! I'd never met a king before. I guessed from the look in his eyes that I wasn't there to talk about the neighborhood or how things were going in Rabbah—which is where the army was fighting.

He came toward me. I tried to put him off—involved Uriah's name, told him I was ill. "You have wives galore," I said. "Let me go."

I learned one does not argue with a king—not this king, anyway.

He carried me into his bedroom and imposed his love on me, and I went home, to compose myself. And I was careful not to bathe when the king was walking on his roof!

Some weeks went by. Uriah hadn't come home—he was still off fighting—and I began to feel nauseated in the mornings, and I suspected. When I missed two periods I sent a message to David, the king: "Your majesty, I am pregnant."

> The sages say that Bathsheba was different from all of David's other wives. She tells Solomon that none of his father's wives except her ever saw David after they became pregnant. But she forced her way into his presence and slept with him again during the pregnancy so that Solomon would be sure to have the king's looks and strength. (*Numbers Rabbah* 10.4)

I didn't hear from him.

Not until later, after Uriah died, did I learn what the king had done to try and cover up his sin.

When Uriah died, I was beside myself. I had truly loved him. I learned he had been put in the forefront of battle—at King David's order.

It was the king's final act of desperation. He had made other attempts. First he called Uriah back to Jerusalem, on the pretext of wanting to know how the war was going. Then he told him to go home and rest, be with me. Assuming, of course, that we'd have intercourse. Then there'd be no mystery about my being pregnant.

I am told Uriah protested—it wasn't fair to the other soldiers, who were risking their necks fighting, sleeping out in the open fields, for him to go home to a wife and sumptuous food and a soft bed.

The king tried again—got Uriah drunk so it would soften his conscience and he would come home to me. But again Uriah stayed with the servants and would not come home.

Then—my heart still stops, thinking about it—David sent a message to Joab—even gave it to Uriah to deliver!—to put Uriah in the front line of the fighting. Which Joab did. And Uriah died, without our ever seeing each other again.

Oh, I mourned him—not only that I loved him, not only for a good man gone too soon—but that he had been the victim of the king's evil. I mourned for our nation too—to be ruled by so unscrupulous a man.

But I was pregnant, without a husband, without a future. When King David sent for me to be his wife, I went.

But I feared for us. I feared for the child I carried. The prophet Nathan came. He invoked the voice of the Lord, "How can you have done this thing? After all I have done for you, anointing you king, delivering you from Saul, giving you wives and lands and nations. And in secret you have killed a man so you can have his wife! For this evil I will punish you in the eyes of all!"

To his credit David repented. "I have sinned against the Lord."

Nathan said, "God hears you. He will not take your life. But because of what you have done, the life of the child you have conceived in sin will be taken."

I fell into despondency. It was my child, too. And I was blameless.

It was all years ago. The child was born healthy enough, but he fell sick and died. I still think of him. David and I were both terribly distraught.

Now we have another child. I wonder what will become of him. His name is Solomon. *(Martha Whitmore Hickman)*

Bathsheba told Solomon that while all of David's other wives prayed, "Let my child be king," she had prayed, "Let my child love the study of Torah and be wise as a prophet." Later when Solomon was granted a gift from God, it is little wonder that he, too, chose wisdom. His mother had set the example. (*Numbers Rabbah* 10.4)

Tamar

Lured into taking care of her half-brother Amnon because he feigns illness, Tamar is raped, then cast away by him.

The Story

The following occurred some time later. David's son Absalom had a beautiful sister named Tamar, and David's son Amnon fell in love with her. Amnon was so tormented that he became ill with love for his half-sister; for he thought it an impossible thing to approach her since she was a virgin. But Amnon had a friend, a very shrewd man named Jonadab, son of David's brother Shimeah, and he said to Amnon, 'Why are you, the king's son, so low-spirited morning after morning? Will you not tell me?' Amnon told him that he was in love with Tamar, his brother Absalom's sister. Jonadab said to him, 'Take to your bed and pretend to be ill. When your father comes to visit you, say to him, "Please let my sister Tamar come and give me my food. Let her prepare it in front of me, so that I may watch her and then take it from her own hands."' So Amnon lay down and pretended to be ill. When the king came to visit him, he said, 'Sir, let my sister Tamar come and make a few bread-cakes in front of me, and serve them to me with her own hands.'

David sent a message to Tamar in the palace: 'Go to your brother Amnon's quarters and prepare a meal for him.' Tamar came to her brother and found him lying down. She took some dough, kneaded it, and made cakes in front of him; having baked them, she took the pan and turned them out before him. But Amnon refused to eat and ordered everyone out of the room. When they had all gone, he said to Tamar, 'Bring the food over to the recess so that I may eat from your own hands.' Tamar took the cakes she had made and brought them to Amnon her brother in the recess. When she offered them to him, he caught hold of her and said, 'Sister, come to bed with me.' She answered, 'No, my brother, do not dishonour me. Such things are not done in Israel; do not behave so infamously. Where could I go and hide my disgrace? You would sink as low as the most infamous in Israel. Why not speak to the king for me? He will not refuse you leave to marry me.' But he would not listen; he overpowered and raped her.

Then Amnon was filled with intense revulsion; his revulsion for her was stronger than the love he had felt; he said to her, 'Get up and go.' She answered, 'No, this great wrong, your sending me away, is worse than anything else you have done to me.' He would not listen to her; he summoned the servant who attended him and said,

129

'Rid me of this woman; put her out and bolt the door after her.' The servant turned her out and bolted the door. She had on a long robe with sleeves, the usual dress of unmarried princesses. Tamar threw ashes over her head, tore the robe that she was wearing, put her hand on her head, and went away, sobbing as she went.

Her brother Absalom asked her, 'Has your brother Amnon been with you?

Keep this to yourself; he is your brother. Do not take it to heart.' Forlorn and desolate, Tamar remained in her brother Absalom's house. When King David heard the whole story he was very angry; but he would not hurt Amnon because he was his eldest son and he loved him. Absalom did not speak a single word to Amnon, friendly or unfriendly, but he hated him for having dishonoured his sister Tamar.

Comments on the Story

Just as the narrative of David and Bathsheba shows that the king's mistreatment of his subjects led to suffering and death, so too does the story of Amnon and Tamar link the abuse of an innocent woman to a greater tragedy of bloodshed in Israel, precipitated by David's sons. Amnon, David's son who rapes his half-sister Tamar and later refuses to honor his responsibility to her, incurs the wrath of Absalom, Tamar's full brother. The revenge that Absalom takes on Amnon escalates into a war with David over the throne. In the course of the conflict, soldiers allied to David and to Absalom are killed. David loses both sons, Amnon by Absalom's hand and Absalom at the hand of David's commander, Joab. Tamar, the woman abused and abandoned, finds no justice. The entire nation of Israel is threatened by political instability and factional rebellion.

The account begins with telling references to the familial relationships. By identifying Tamar as Absalom's sister (instead of, for example, David's daughter), reference is made to the bond that will inspire Absalom's revenge. Amnon, also identified as David's son, shares in the family relationship as Absalom and Tamar's half brother. Amnon is so enamored of Tamar that he becomes ill. This theme of sickness continues throughout the narrative. Amnon's clever friend Jonadab, also a family member (David's nephew), helps Amnon plot to have intercourse with the virgin Tamar. Following Jonadab's advice and pretending to be ill, Amnon receives a visit from King David and insists that Tamar be sent to care and cook for him. The Hebrew word used for "breadcakes" (v. 6) is sexually suggestive. *Levivot* comes from the root word *lev*, meaning heart. Thus Amnon asks that Tamar make him, literally, "heart-shaped cakes."

David sends the orders to Tamar, who obeys. Amnon's plotting continues. Pretending to be unable to eat, he dismisses all in the household. Once alone, he summons Tamar to his bedside to feed him. She arrives, discovering that it is his lust that he wants fed. He seizes her and, calling her "sister," tells her to lie with him. She refuses, and for the first time in the narrative we hear her speak. Composed yet insistent, she chastises him for desiring to commit such a crime. Her reference to the exact nature of the crime is uncertain. There were laws in Israel that forbade intercourse between siblings and half-siblings of the same father, but it is not clear whether they were in effect at this time. If they were, the sin might refer to incest as well as to rape. It is possible that the narrator assumes the laws were in effect because the account is replete with brother and sister references, appropriate for a description of incest. Tamar continues to protest; she says that if Amnon would ask David for her, she would be given to him. Thus it appears that the king had the right or custom to override prohibitions of sibling marriages. Whether or not the crime is considered incest as well as rape, it is clear that Tamar is assaulted. Yet even this rape is not the end of Amnon's violation of Tamar.

In the next scene Amnon's love for Tamar quickly is transformed into hatred for his victim. Demanding that Tamar leave his home, she again reminds him of the law and his responsibility. If an unmarried woman were raped, the man would be obligated to marry her. As repugnant as this sounds to a modern audience, the idea was that the man had a responsibility to the woman who was no longer a virgin and presumably no longer a candidate for marriage with another man. In a society where women were dependent on their fathers and husbands for support as well as status, there were few options for an unmarried woman. Indeed, Tamar's words illustrate the importance of this law, "this great wrong, your sending me away, is worse than anything else you have done to me" (v. 16). Refusing to listen to her, Amnon enlists his servant to cast her out. The scene is moving. Tamar is in mourning, using the customary symbols to mark her grief: ashes and a torn garment. The narrator calls attention to her dress as the type that virgin princesses wore, a status that has been violently taken from her.

Tamar's violation is never addressed. Even Absalom seems to dismiss his sister's grief, although he does tell her to stay in his home. David's love for Amnon prompts him to refuse to punish Amnon or force him to marry Tamar; apparently he has little regard for his daughter and shows no responsibility for her plight when she stays in Absalom's home. The narrator describes her dismal situation; she is "forlorn and desolate" there (v. 20). Indeed, living in a culture where women have no esteem if they do not have children, Tamar is sentenced to a lifetime of suffering. It is ironic that the one who can uphold the law, David, ignores it, whereas the powerless Tamar has spoken eloquently about the necessity for justice. Absalom harbors hatred and resentment toward Amnon, but his later act of murder and attempt to seize the throne show that he was more concerned with revenge than with Tamar's plight or with justice. In fact, his revenge will have no impact on Tamar's situation. Still, a hint of his care for Tamar is indicated later when the reader learns that Absalom names one of his daughters Tamar (14:27).

David and the entire Israelite populace pay the price for the sin against the innocent Tamar. Once the rape was committed there were opportunities to mitigate its continuing effects, but none were taken. Amnon refused to marry Tamar, and King David refused to enforce the law or to punish him. Absalom's revenge leads to Amnon's murder and Absalom's battle with David for the throne. When David secures the throne and Absalom is killed, yet another factional rebellion occurs. The point of the tragedy is clear. When God's laws are ignored, an individual may suffer greatly, and even an entire nation may be at risk.

Retelling the Story

ALL DAVID'S CHILDREN (ACTING SCRIPT)

Scene 1: AMNON *and* JONADAB *are sitting in the dim light of a bar. Each has a drink sitting on the bar in front of him.* AMNON *is obviously disturbed, while* JONADAB *attempts to console him.*

AMNON: I feel like I could throw up, and it's been this way for weeks.

JONADAB: Maybe you shouldn't have any more to drink.

AMNON: It's not that.

JONADAB: Well, then maybe you should go to the doctor.

AMNON: It's not that either, stupid. I just can't get Tamar off my mind. When I see her it just does me in. I think about her all the time. She is such a babe.

JONADAB: So? What's stopping you?

AMNON: You mean besides the fact that she's my half-sister.

JONADAB: So you would just be keeping it in the family. *(He smiles a lurid smile.)*

AMNON: Yeah, but she's a real untouchable. I mean seriously, she's a good girl in the worst sense of the word. I could never get near her.

JONADAB: Never say never, my man. You said you were under the weather? Let you sickness work for you. Tell your old man that you're in bed, so sick you can't move and ask if sweetcakes can't drop by with a little chicken soup and dry toast. Then when you have her in your clutches, just let nature take its course.

AMNON: *(Stands and reaches into his pocket for a quarter.)* You are a genius. I'll be right back. *(Exits to telephone.)*

JONADAB: *(Shouting after him)* Hey, jerk, call from home. You don't want him to hear U2 singing you to sleep in the background.

(Cut to commercial.)

• • •

Scene 2: AMNON is lying in bed, sheets pulled up to just under his chin. He is wearing a pajama shirt and feigns illness. The doorbell rings.

AMNON: *(Weakly)* Come in.

TAMAR: *(Enters carrying a tray with food. She is strikingly beautiful but modestly dressed. Her voice exudes concern.)* Well, how's the patient? Our father tells me you are under the weather.

AMNON: Not doing any better, I'm afraid. Did you come alone?

TAMAR: Of course, silly. We don't want anybody else taking a chance on getting what you've got, now do we? Here, we'll have you feeling much better before you know it. *(She sets the tray on the bed.)*

{AMNON: That's what I'm counting on. *(He grasps her arm.)*

TAMAR: *(Still innocent of his intentions)* What are you doing? Have you no shame? You are my own father's son. Is it that you want me to marry you? Is that it? *(Clearly desperate)* Ask the king, he might agree. Only let me go.

AMNON: *(Pulling her onto the bed and him.)* Listen, sister, this is what I've wanted to do for months.

TAMAR: *(Terrified, attempting to pull herself up.)* No, don't!

(Cut to commercial.)

As Tamar left Amnon's rooms, the story says, she tore her clothing and placed ashes on her head, all signs of her grief and humiliation. Some of the sages say that she was left so ashamed by her half-brother's assault that she also covered her head with a hood so no one could see who she was. This is another clear example of the victim bearing the shame rather than the perpetrator. (*Numbers Rabbah* 9.33)

• • •

Scene 3: AMNON is sitting in bed wearing no pajama shirt, but is wearing the bottoms. He is smoking a cigarette. Cut to TAMAR cowering in a corner of the room, wrapped only in the sheet from the bed. Her eyes are red and swollen from crying, and her voice betrays the hurt she has experienced.

• • •

Some rabbis say that Amnon would have been better off if King David had punished him more severely when he learned Amnon had violated his own sister. They suggest that, if stronger measures were taken then, Amnon might have avoided his violent end, orchestrated by his half-brother (and Tamar's full brother) Absalom. (*Ecclesiastes Rabbah* 4.2(5)

AMNON: You know, I don't know why I ever thought you were so beautiful. You look like hell right now.

TAMAR: *(Attempts to speak, but her words stop in her throat in a guttural sob.)*

AMNON: What? What was that? What did you call me?

TAMAR: *(Hardly audible.)* Son of David, you have committed a great wrong against me.

AMNON: Why, you little tramp. I hate you more now than I wanted you before. Get out of here.

TAMAR: *(Stumbles as she rises, picks up her dress and exits.)* Great wrong, great wrong.

When the sages draw up a list of the most notorious sinners in history, Amnon is among them. (*Ecclesiastes Rabbah* 7.27[1])

(Cut to commercial.)

(Michael E. Williams)

The Wise Woman

At Joab's urging, a woman goes to David and tells him a story intended to convince David to let Absalom back into his good graces.

The Story

Joab son of Zeruiah saw the king longed in his heart for Absalom, so he sent for a wise woman from Tekoah and said to her, 'Pretend to be a mourner; put on mourning garb, go without anointing yourself, and behave like a woman who has been bereaved these many days. Then go to the king and repeat what I tell you.' He told her exactly what she was to say.

When the woman from Tekoah came into the king's presence, she bowed to the ground in homage and cried, 'Help, your majesty!' The king asked, 'What is it?' She answered, 'Sir, I am a widow; my husband is dead. I had two sons; they came to blows out in the country where there was no one to part them, and one struck the other and killed him. Now, sir, the kinsmen have confronted me with the demand, "Hand over the one who killed his brother, so that we can put him to death for taking his brother's life, and so cut off the succession." If they do this, they will stamp out my last live ember or descendant on the earth.' 'Go home,' said the king to the woman, 'and I shall settle your case.'

But the woman continued, 'The guilt be on me, your majesty, and on my father's house; let the king and his throne be blameless.' The king said, 'If anyone says anything more to you, bring him to me and he will not trouble you again.' Then the woman went on, 'Let your majesty call upon the LORD your God, to prevent the next-of-kin from doing their worst and destroying my son.' The king swore, 'As the LORD lives, not a hair of your son's head shall fall to the ground.'

The woman then said, 'May I add one word more, your majesty?' 'Say on,' said the king. So she continued, 'How then could it enter your head to do this same wrong to God's people? By the decision you have pronounced, your majesty, you condemn yourself in that you have refused to bring back the one you banished. We shall all die; we shall be like water that is spilt on the ground and lost; but God will spare the man who does not sent himself to keep the outlaw in banishment.

'I came to say this to your majesty because the people have threatened me: I thought, "If I can only speak to the king, perhaps he will attend to my case; for he will listen, and he will save me from anyone who is seeking to cut off me and my son together from God's own possession." I thought too that the words of my lord the king would be a comfort to me; for your majesty is like the angel of God and can decide between right and wrong. May the LORD your God be with you!'

The king said to the woman, 'Tell me no lies: I shall now ask you a question.' 'Let your majesty speak,' she said. The king asked, 'Is the hand of Joab behind you in all this?' 'Your life upon it, sir!' she answered. 'When your majesty asks a question, there is no way round it, right or left. Yes, your servant Joab did prompt me; it was he who put the whole story into my mouth. He did it to give a new turn to this affair. Your majesty is as wise as the angel of God and knows all that goes on in the land.'

The king said to Joab, 'You have my consent; go and bring back the young man Absalom.' Then Joab humbly prostrated himself, took leave of the king with a blessing, and said, 'Now I know that I have found favour with your majesty, because you have granted my humble petition.' Joab went at once to Geshur and brought Absalom to Jerusalem. But the king said, 'Let him go to his own quarters; he shall not come into my presence.' So Absalom repaired to his own quarters and did not enter the king's presence.

In all Israel no man was so much admired for his beauty as Absalom; from the crown of his head to the sole of his foot he was without flaw. When he cut his hair (as had to be done every year, for he found it heavy), it weighed two hundred shekels by the royal standard. Three sons were born to Absalom, and a daughter named Tamar, who became a very beautiful woman.

Absalom lived in Jerusalem for two whole years without entering the king's presence. Then he summoned Joab, intending to send a message by him to the king, but Joab refused to come; he sent for him a second time, but he still refused. Absalom said to his servants, 'You know that Joab has a field next to mine with barley growing in it; go and set fire to it.' When Absalom's servants set afire to the field, Joab promptly came to Absalom in his own quarters and demanded, 'Why have your servants set fire to my field?' Absalom answered, 'I had sent for you to come here, so that I could ask you to give the king this message from me: "Why did I leave Geshur? It would be better for me if I were still there. Let me now come into your majesty's presence and, if I have done any wrong, put me to death." ' When Joab went to the king and told him, he summoned Absalom, who came and prostrated himself humbly, and the king greeted him with a kiss.

Comments on the Story

This account of the unnamed woman from Tekoa who prompts King David to reconsider his banishment of his son Absalom after Absalom's murder of Amnon takes place immediately following the account of the rape of Tamar. Just as Tamar spoke about the necessity of justice for herself, so also the woman from Tekoa speaks about the need for David to act justly and mercifully toward his son Absalom so that the entire nation will not suffer due to the dissolution of the royal family. In both these accounts it is significant that women, members of the bottom rung of a patriarchal society, must cajole men in positions of power—even the king—to follow God's laws.

Prompted by Joab, David's commander, the woman from Tekoa pretends to be a widow suffering the same tragedy as David. She claims to have had two sons—the first murdered by the other, and the second fleeing for his life from kin who seek revenge. Although the essence of the story was given to her by Joab, her method of relating the story reveals her courage and her wisdom. She seizes the king's attention by shouting "Help!" In a passionate speech, she relates her alleged situation, directly quoting the threat to her living son, heightening its impact. She states the consequences of the threat in such a way that underscores the importance for every Israelite to have descendants. David responds that he will solve her desperate problem.

Assurance from the king does not stop her from pleading her case further, thereby showing David the similarity to his own situation. She continues her conversation with him three separate times, then, courageously, makes the king realize that his refusal to send for Absalom will have consequences for the entire nation. She undercuts any rage David might feel from her comparison by appealing to the moral rectitude of the king's decisions. Ironically, the reader knows of David's past crimes and his failure to act upon the problem with Absalom. When David surmises that Joab has initiated the woman's speech, she does not lose her composure, but continues to flatter him by saying that David is so wise to figure it out! If only the truly wise woman's words were followed. Although David takes the woman's advice and allows Absalom to return to Jerusalem, he refuses to see him for two years, allowing the problem to escalate. In addition, when Joab has the opportunity to bring father and son together, he delays. David, noted for his wisdom, acts foolishly; Joab, who sent for the woman from Tekoa, has acted irresponsibly. In contrast, the unassuming woman from Tekoa acts with true wisdom. The reader is challenged to reconsider his or her assumptions about the location of wise judgment.

Retelling the Story

Joab asked about me in the town market, for he had heard I was a good actress and could think on my feet. At first when he told me what I would have to do I said no. How could I lie to our king? And if the king found out that Joab had coached me and told me what to say, how would he behave? Of course, King David is beloved, just, and fair. But everyone knows he was overcome with grief at the business among Tamar, Amnon, and his favorite son, Absalom, so maybe he wasn't ready to bring Absalom back to the fold.

Josephus says that the wise woman Joab called from Tekoa to talk to the king was very old. Does he associate wisdom with age, or does he think the maladies of old age will make the king more inclined to hear her story? We do not know. But the woman in Josephus's version of the story thanks the king for taking pity on her because of her age. (Josephus, *Antiquities*, VII, 8.4)

Joab not only offered me money, he appealed to my sense of love, too. Why should a father cut off his favorite child? The period of mourning was over, Absalom should be admitted again to the king's court. The king, Joab explained, was just as human as the rest of us. He wanted his son back again—indeed, the rumors were he was pining away for Absalom. But King David couldn't bring himself to send for Absalom. Men are like that sometimes. They stick so strongly to their principles and forget that the heart is what's important in these matters.

My friend Rizpah had sent Joab to me. She knows more about the ins and outs of the king's family than anyone I've met. Just before Joab came to see me, Rizpah rushed to my house to tell me to expect him. She'd known his mother, she said, and trusted his good intentions. And she told me that only good could come of my doing what he asked.

So I said I'd go to King David. Joab gave me a script, and I spent three days memorizing it until not only I but everyone in my family knew it by heart. My husband wasn't too excited about my going, especially as I was going to tell the king I was a widow. But I appreciated the drama of that art; it made the whole scenario more plausible.

The guards ushered me into the king's receiving room. It was beautiful, just as I had imagined it. And there sat David, on a throne on a small raised platform. He was very nice about the whole thing, listened intently to my story, not distracting or condescending at all. I played the part as best I could—even putting a tremor in my voice when I described how the death of my second son would "quench the last ember remaining to me, and leave my husband without name or remnant upon the earth." It wasn't too difficult—I've seen tragedy in my time. Who hasn't?

The king told me to go home, that he would issue an order on my behalf, that he would make sure my son would not be harmed. Then I improvised a bit. I wanted to make sure King David didn't miss the relevance of the predicament I posed to him. I may have been a little too direct, but I wanted to make my point. "Why, then, do you not bring back your own banished son?" I asked him.

I thought he was going to get angry that I, a commoner, had the effrontery to question his actions. Instead his face fell for a moment, and then I saw him get a glimmering as to what the charade was all about. He asked me directly, "Is Joab in league with you?"

Of course, I had to admit the whole thing, but I made sure to do it respectfully, flattering the king as much as possible. And Joab was right. King David was capable of thinking with his heart. As I stood there, King David

> In Josephus the woman tells David that she cannot trust his decision concerning her sons as long as he has a son in exile for killing his half-brother. When the king hears this he realizes that this story is really the work of Joab. (Josephus, *Antiquities,* VII.8.4)

sent for Joab and told him to bring Absalom back to Jerusalem. Then he sent me home with presents for my family. I'll never forget him on that day—sad and vulnerable, wise and forgiving.

Later I heard it was another two years before the king could bear to see his son, but that's the way with men—they don't trust their feelings. All those "principles" they have to live by, when we women know immediately the right thing to do. But I guess that's why God made both of us, men and women. Every so often we have to remind them to follow their hearts, and I guess once in a while men remind women to use their heads. *(Betty Lehrman)*

Prostitutes

Solomon judges between two women, each of whom claims that a child is hers, and decides who the real mother is on the basis of one of the women's compassion toward the child.

The Story

Two women who were prostitutes approached the king at that time, and as they stood before him one said, 'My lord, this woman and I share a house, and I gave birth to a child when she was there with me. On the third day after my baby was born she too gave birth to a child. We were alone; no one else was with us in the house; only the two of us were there.

During the night this woman's child died because she lay on it, and she got up in the middle of the night, took my baby from my side and while I, your servant, was asleep, and laid it on her bosom, putting her dead child on mine. When I got up in the morning to feed my baby, I found him dead; but when I looked at him closely, I found that it was not the child that I had borne.' The other woman broke in, 'No, the living child is mine; yours is the dead one,' while the first insisted, 'No, the dead child is yours; mine is the living one.' So they went on arguing before the king.

The king thought to himself, 'One of them says, "This is my child, the living one; yours is the dead one." The other says, "No, it is your child that is dead and mine that is alive." ' Then he said, 'Fetch me a sword.' When a sword was brought, the king gave the order: 'Cut the living child in two and give half to one woman and half to the other.' At this the woman who was the mother of the living child, moved with love for her child, said to the king, 'Oh, sir, let her have the baby! Whatever you do, do not kill it.' The other said, 'Let neither of us have it; cut it in two.' The king then spoke up: 'Give the living baby to the first woman,' he said; 'do not kill it. She is its mother.' When Israel heard the judgment which the king had given, they all stood in awe of him; for they saw that he possessed wisdom from God for administering justice.

Comments on the Story

The account of Solomon's distribution of justice to the two unnamed prostitutes is placed in the context of the beginning of Solomon's reign. It hearkens back to Solomon's prayer for wisdom and looks forward to his division of the kingdom into districts to supply the throne with provisions and labor. Although its primary purpose is to establish the wisdom of Solomon, it provides insight into the lives of prostitutes in Israelite culture and into the humanity of all people, even those despised by society.

The opening scene is arresting in its simple statement that two prostitutes "approached the king" (v. 16). The ability of people of such low social standing to have an audience with the king demonstrates the narrator's belief that Solomon was a champion of all Israelites. The story is famous: two women give birth to sons, and when one woman's child dies, she takes the living child from the unsuspecting mother, replacing it with her dead son. Appropriately, the woman who will prove to be the true mother of the living baby speaks to Solomon. Her description of the situation points to a seemingly unsolvable problem. How could anyone determine who was telling the truth when there were no witnesses? Twice she states that they were alone (v. 18). In addition, because prostitutes live under constant suspicion, the reader might assume that neither woman can be trusted. Within the first woman's speech, however, are clues to her honesty and strength of character, although they cannot yet be confirmed until Solomon's test. Her initial statement describing the background of the incident is uncontested by the second woman. They shared a house (perhaps an indication of their poverty or a cipher for a brothel?), and she had given birth to a child three days before the second woman. Thus she had three days to know her child and be certain of his identity. She speaks to the king with the necessary decorum—using terms such as "my lord" (v. 17) and "your servant" (v. 20). She refers to her maternal care for her child; for example, she awoke to feed her baby.

In contrast, when the second woman speaks, she quarrels with the first woman; she does not address the king. The suspense continues. Solomon summarizes the situation correctly, but gives a shocking order by sending for a sword. The narrator slows the account (with a description of the sword being brought and the king giving the order), and the reader must wonder for whom the sword is meant. The first woman? The second woman? Both? After all, the women continue to quarrel before the king. When the action resumes, Solomon's words are arresting: Kill the innocent baby! Is it justice to give half a dead baby to each woman? Is this the king's wisdom? The first woman immediately speaks up and is willing to give the baby to the second woman if Solomon will spare his life. The second woman agrees with Solomon's judgment, showing her disregard for the baby's life. Only at this point in the suspense does the reader discover that Solomon's order was a test to reveal the real mother. Israel marvels at his wisdom and acknowledges that it comes from God.

This account both confirms and challenges society's expectations of prostitutes. The second woman's characterization is based on the stereotype of the harlot who will lead men astray by her lies, deceit, and uncontrolled sexuality. She carelessly lies on her baby. She steals another woman's child. She quarrels and lies before the king. She is willing to accept the execution of an innocent baby! This depiction reflects society's worst opinions of prostitutes. At the same time, the first woman is portrayed as a caring mother and a courageous woman. She is willing to address the king, and she speaks poignantly of the event. She reacts passionately when her baby is to be killed. Although her status would be elevated by having a child, especially a son, she does not think of the loss of her status and the elevation of the second woman's position if the boy were to be given to her. She thinks only of the baby's life. Because of this characterization, the reader is challenged to reconsider the stereotype of prostitutes and ponder the humanity of this woman.

Retelling the Story

It was back in the forties, around 1946 I'd say. Many of the men were still overseas, but there were enough home already that a lot of babies were being born, all of a sudden. We had to double up most of our patients, even when they'd requested private rooms. There was a nursing shortage (as usual) and because of the war effort they'd never constructed that new wing they'd planned. So everyone was tense and overworked.

The university's women's hospital was always known for excellent care, don't get me wrong. We were affiliated with the Harvard University Medical School; the care that premature babies got there was among the best in the country. We had well-equipped labor rooms, and state-of-the-art delivery room equipment. The waiting rooms weren't bad, either, although why the new fathers always had to smoke when waiting for a little one I never figured out.

It is told that Ruth, the great-great-grandmother of Solomon, did not die until she saw his wisdom demonstrated as he sat in judgment in the case of the two prostitutes. (*Ruth Rabbah 2.2*)

After the births an orderly would take the babies to be weighed and measured, and then they'd come to the nursery. The women were brought up to our floor at about the same time. If they were awake enough we'd give them some instruction in caring for themselves postpartum, and talk with them about what to expect in the hospital. They stayed in the hospital a week or two back then, and we nurses took care of the newborns.

I'd just come on my shift when two babies were brought into the nursery. They looked very similar: the same coloring, the same bit of black hair. We always check their tags when they come in, as well as any instructions the obstetricians have written down about them. I noticed the ankle tag on one of the babies was missing, and saw a tag on the floor. So I put it on the bare ankle and tended to some other newborns. There were twelve babies there that night, and just two of us on the floor.

A few hours later I noticed that the coloring on one of the newborns was very yellow. It's easy these days to do something about jaundice, but back then we didn't know very much. We did what we could for him, but the poor thing didn't pull through. We checked the identification tag on him, and went to inform the mother. She cried and carried on and said she just wanted to see him one more time. Well, it wasn't really regulations in those days, but the other nurse brought her in to see the little fellow. That's when things got complicated.

The mother started screaming that the dead baby wasn't her child, that another baby was really hers, and we'd gotten them mixed up. We looked at the other, healthy baby who looked so similar and sure enough, he had no tag on him. I examined the dead child more closely and found two tags on his ankle, and no way to know which was the tag I'd found and put on him, and which was the one from the doctor at the time of birth.

Meanwhile, the other mother had gotten involved. She, of course, insisted that the living baby was hers. We calmed everyone down and ran blood tests, but the findings were inconclusive. We couldn't do DNA testing or any of those fancy procedures back then.

It was the senior nurse on the floor, Jeanne, who figured it out. She heard some story, she said, about two mothers who both claimed the same child. She brought both mothers into the nursery and picked the baby up from its bassinet. Then she uncurled its little fingers and placed one tiny hand around the finger of one of the mothers and the other hand around the other woman's finger. She looked really fierce, and she told the two of them if they wanted their baby they'd have to fight for him. "Pull," she told them. "And the one who pulls the hardest is the true mother."

Some of the rabbis say that the prostitutes who appeared in Solomon's court were really seductive spirits. If they had really been prostitutes, say these sages, they would not have cared enough for their children to go to court. Others disagree and claim that they were, indeed, prostitutes and that even a prostitute can have compassion on her own child. (*Songs of Songs Rabbah* 1.1[10]; *Ecclesiastes Rabbah* 10.15[1-16])

One of the mothers hung on tight and pulled, and the baby began to cry. The other mother let go. "Don't hurt him!" she pleaded. "Take him, but don't hurt him!"

Jeanne took the baby and gave him to the second mother. It was obvious to all of us that she was his real mother.

We felt sorry for the woman who lost her child. But that's life, sometimes. We got a note from that second woman a few weeks after she left the hospital. She and her little boy were doing fine. I often wonder what happened to him and to his mother. As for Jeanne, she got a nice promotion. A few years later she left nursing and went to law school. I even heard she made federal judge. *(Betty Lehrman)*

The Widow of Sidon

A widow shows a risky kindness to the prophet Elijah and is rewarded when her son's life is given back.

The Story

Elijah the Tishbite from Tisbe in Gilead said to Ahab, 'I swear by the life of the LORD the God of Israel, whose servant I am, that there will be neither dew nor rain these coming years unless I give the word.' Then the word of the LORD came to him: 'Leave this place, turn eastwards, and go into hiding in the wadi of Kerith east of the Jordan. You are to drink from the stream, and I have commanded the ravens to feed you there.' Elijah did as the LORD had told him: he went and stayed in the wadi of Kerith east of the Jordan, and the ravens brought him bread and meat morning and evening, and he drank from the stream.

After a while the stream dried up, for there had been no rain in the land. Then the word of the LORD came to him: 'Go now to Zarephath, a village of Sidon, and stay there; I have commanded a widow there to feet you.' He went off to Zarephath, and when he reached the entrance to the village, he saw a widow gathering sticks. He called to her, 'Please bring me a little water in a pitcher to drink.' As she went to fetch it, he called after her, 'Bring me, please, a piece of bread as well.' But she answered, 'As the LORD your God lives, I have no food baked, only a handful of flour in a jar and a little oil in a flask. I am just gathering two or three sticks to go and cook it for my son and myself before we die.' 'Have no fear,' said Elijah; 'go and do as you have said. But first make me a small cake from what you have and bring it out to me, and after that make something for your son and yourself. For this the word of the LORD the God of Israel: The jar of flour will not give out, nor the flask of oil fail, until the LORD sends rain on the land.' She went and did as Elijah had said, and there was food for him and for her and her family for a long time. The jar of flour did not give out, nor did the flask of oil fail, as the word of the LORD foretold through Elijah.

Afterwards the son of the woman, the owner of the house, fell ill and was in a very bad way, until at last his breathing stopped. The woman said to Elijah, 'What made you interfere, you man of God? You came here to bring my sins to light and cause my son's death!' 'Give me your son,' he said. He took the boy from her arms and carried him up to the roof-chamber where his lodging was, and laid him on his bed. He called out to the LORD, 'LORD my God, is this your care for the widow with whom I lodge, that you have been

147

so cruel to her son?' Then he breathed deeply on the child three times and called to the LORD, 'I pray, LORD my God, let the breath of life return to the body of this child.' The LORD listened to Elijah's cry, and the breath of life returned to the child's body, and he revived.

Elijah lifted him and took him down from the roof-chamber into the house, and giving him to his mother he said, 'Look, your son is alive.' She said to Elijah, 'Now I know for certain that you are a man of God and that the word of the LORD on your lips is truth.'

Comments on the Story

The account of the prophet Elijah and the widow from Sidon is given in the context of the rule of King Ahab in Israel in the eighth century B.C.E. The editorial judgment on Ahab is harsh: "Ahab son of Omri did evil in the sight of the LORD more than all who were before him" (16:30). Besides his altercations with Ahab, Elijah also contended with Ahab's wife, Jezebel. Jezebel, an outsider from Sidon, had many of Elijah's associates killed and plotted to slay Elijah. It was she, however, who came to an infamous end. In contrast to Jezebel, the unnamed woman from Sidon who encounters Elijah's miracles is a model of faith for Israel.

The setting of the narrative is dire: Elijah has proclaimed a drought for Israel. Not only is this threatening for the people, but Elijah himself is implicitly threatened by the king for invoking this punishment, and the LORD must protect him. First Elijah flees to a stream where ravens feed him. In the past, some commentators thought the Hebrew word *orebim* ("ravens") must have been a misreading of *arebim* ("Arabs") because of the incongruity of ravens feeding a human. But the point of many of Elijah's and his successor Elisha's narratives is precisely the miraculous happenings God provides through them. The feeding by the ravens is a foreshadowing of the miracle of the flour and oil for the well-being of the Sidonian woman.

Just as it was important for Elijah to learn that he would be fed by ravens near a stream, so also it is striking that he is sent to foreign territory to seek refuge. Ironically, the city to which he turns is Sidon, located in the country of Jezebel, the woman who will seek to kill Elijah! The person who will provide for Elijah is of low social standing; she is a foreigner, a woman, and a widow. Such a woman is often without means, and the Hebrew Bible frequently includes texts to remind the community of its responsibility to care for widows and orphans. When Elijah encounters the woman for the first time, she is gathering sticks, whose significance for the preparation of what she thinks will be her last meal will soon be seen. Elijah asks her for water, and she immediately complies, showing her willingness to help a stranger. When, however, Elijah asks for bread as well, she recites her predicament: She has only a tiny amount of flour and oil and is gathering the sticks to make a fire in order to cook the last meal for herself and her son. When Elijah insists that God will not allow "the jar of flour" to be depleted or the "flask of oil" (v. 14) to be spent until rain comes again, she complies.

In both instances of providing water and bread, we do not hear her words, but her silent trust of Elijah is noteworthy. She provides the bread when Elijah speaks of God's word; she does not wait for a sign of proof. The Sidonian woman accepts the word of a prophet of Israel who speaks in the name of Israel's God. Already she shows more faith than the leaders of Israel, who will plot against him. Still, she does not acknowledge the miracle with words or address Elijah after the food is provided.

The account continues with the second episode concerning the death of her son and his revival by Elijah. It may be that this account was originally separate from the story of the feeding (she is now described as the owner of the house, and the residence has an upper structure—perhaps not appropriate references for a widow), but in any case the narrator brings the two scenes together to show the woman's recognition of Elijah and her faith in the God of Israel.

When the widow's son dies, she has lost everything; not only has she lost her only loved one, but she has become still more destitute with the loss of her provider. This time she calls out to Elijah as "man of God," but she connects her son's death with her own sins and blames Elijah for coming into her life. Poignantly, the woman is holding her dead son when the reader learns that Elijah removes him from her arms to take him up to his room. Elijah's call to God is striking in its honesty: How could God be so cruel to the woman who is caring for him? Elijah prays for the restoration of the boy's life, and God answers the prayer.

When Elijah restores the son to his mother, she expresses her faith. She confirms that Elijah is a man of God, and for the first time she specifies that the God of Israel's words are with him. This foreign woman thus serves as a model of how the faithful Israel should act toward Elijah, the prophet of the LORD. Facing starvation and possibly drought, she was willing to provide water for Elijah. Promised that God would see that her meager rations would not run out, she prepared bread for him. Discovering her dead son, she recognizes her own sin and makes the connection of Elijah's presence and God's judgment, an association that Ahab and Jezebel refuse to make. Finally, given her restored son, she states her unqualified faith in Elijah and in the God of Israel.

The account of the widow and Elijah is the first of several miracle stories of Elijah and his successor Elisha that involve women. These women are helped by the prophets precisely because they represent those who have the least voice in Israel. They are also models of faith. Some foreign, others native, they accept Elijah as God's prophet, trust in his word, and believe in God in spite of experiencing some of the worst political and social problems in ancient Israel's history.

Retelling the Story

"You just can't tell about people; that's what I think. They seem totally crazy, or unreasonably demanding—or both—and then on the other hand sometimes they seem to have arcane powers—or a direct line to God. How do I know?"

The widows' support group was gathered for its usual Wednesday meeting. "Tell us about it, Myra," Dorothea said. "But first, is your little boy all right? I know he had a terrible sick spell last week. Some of us heard about it, and we were worried."

"You and me both," she said. "But that's part of the story." And she launched into her tale.

"You know how dry it's been around here—not near enough rain?"

They all nodded—yes, they knew.

"Well, last week I was out at the edge of town, right there by my house, picking up a little kindling—that's one thing the drought has done for us, given us some dry wood—when this vagrant—I don't know how else to describe him—called out to me, 'Lady, I'm thirsty. Could you spare a drink of water?' "

She looked up. Yes, they shared her consternation.

The rabbis contend that giving alms to the poor or food to the hungry is such a powerful action that it brings with it the resurrection of the dead before its time. By this they do not just mean simply saving the life of the one being helped. They offer for an example the widow who fed Elijah, a poor stranger, though she was at the point of the last meal for herself and her son. Her compassion created the conditions for her son to be raised back to life. (*Song of Songs Rabbah* 2.5[3])

"Well, it seemed a little odd—not the safest thing in the world—but I thought, *Sure. It won't hurt to share my water.* So I'm carrying over a cup of water, and he calls out, 'How about a piece of bread, too? Could you bring me a piece of bread?'

"I was a little exasperated. *This is too much,* I thought. 'I don't have any bread,' I hollered back. 'I have only a smidgen of flour and a little oil. I was just gathering some kindling so I could build a fire and use what little I have to bake bread for my son and myself, so we don't starve.'

"Did that faze him? No. He said, 'Well, before you make any for your son and yourself, make me a little bit, then do yours.' I was about to tell him nothing doing and who did he think he was anyway, when he said something like, 'The God of Israel promises you'll have all the flour and oil you need for as long as this drought lasts.'

"I know this sounds crazy, and it was partly the way he said it, but I thought, *Well, maybe he's on to something. Maybe I'd better not fool with this guy.* So I did what he said, and, believe it or not, we had plenty of food. For several days." There was a buzz in the room, and she heard fragments of conversation—"Can you imagine?" "What could it mean?"

She went on, "I wondered what kind of power this man had."

They shook their heads in shared astonishment—and a little bit of envy. They wished somebody would come and promise them endless supplies.

"But that's not all," she said, and this time her voice shook. "My little boy— the one you'd heard was sick?" she looked up.

"Yes." They were listening.

"My little boy got terribly sick. My first thought was that this stranger with his powers of filling empty food jars knew every stray thought I'd ever had, every little compromise with truth, and he was paying me back by making my child sick. Sick unto death," she said, wanting to be sure they knew just how sick the boy had been.

They nodded in unison. News of sick children traveled fast in their circle. "So then what?" one of them asked, brushing a strand of hair from her forehead.

"I pleaded with the man, 'What have I done to you that you are repaying my sins by killing my son? What is it to you?'"

Again they nodded. A good question.

"He said, 'Bring me your son.' And I did, right away, though my little one wasn't even breathing." Her voice sank to a whisper. "I was sure he was dead."

She waited while that sank in. "And this man, this vagrant, who had invoked the name of God, invoked the name of God again. He prayed." She took a deep breath, as though even now she could hardly believe what she'd seen with her own eyes. "Then, with his own body, he stretched out along the body of my son. It was like a healing touch, or faith healing. I don't know what it was. But right there, his whole body (I hoped he was clean but I wasn't about to question) pressed against the body of my little boy, and he prayed, 'Revive him. Give him back the breath of life.'"

The widow first thought that she had enough for herself, her son, and the prophet to eat because she had showed such compassion on a stranger. Then when her son died she blamed herself, thinking her good deeds to be nothing compared to a prophet of God. The sages say that Elijah raised her son to show her that taking credit or blame is a worthless activity. Some even say that the boy whose life was saved grew up to be the prophet Jonah. (Ginzberg, IV, 196-97)

She looked around the circle of her friends, those persons with whom she had shared some of her darkest hours. She would now share her newfound faith in God with these dear friends. "And my son revived," she said, "and I knew this man spoke the word of the Lord to me." *(Martha Whitmore Hickman)*

Esther

A Hebrew woman, Esther, marries a king and then confronts him about the injustice of one of his advisers toward her people through her acts of wisdom and courage.

The Story

So the King and Haman went to Queen Esther's banquet, and again on that second day over the wine the king said, 'Whatever you ask will be given you, Queen Esther. Whatever you request, up to half my kingdom, it will be granted.' She answered, 'If I have found favour with your majesty, and if it please you, my lord, what I ask is that my own life and the lives of my people be spared. For we have been sold, I and my people, to be destroyed, slain, and exterminated. If it had been a matter of selling us, men and women alike, into slavery, I should have kept silence; for then our plight would not have been such as to injure the king's interest.' King Ahasuerus demanded, 'Who is he, and where is he, who has dared to do such a thing? A ruthless enemy,' she answered, 'this wicked Haman!' Haman stood aghast before the king and queen. In a rage the king rose from the banquet and went into the garden of the pavilion, while Haman remained where he was to plead for his life with Queen Esther; for he saw that in the king's mind his fate was determined. When the king returned from the pavilion garden to the banqueting hall, Haman had flung himself on the couch where Esther was reclining. The king exclaimed, 'Will he even assault the queen in the palace before my very eyes?' The words had no sooner left the king's lips than Haman's face was covered. Habona, one of the eunuchs in attendance on the king, said, 'There is a gallows seventy-five feet high standing at Haman's house; he had it erected for Mordecai, whose evidence once saved your majesty.' 'Let Haman be hanged on it!' said the king. So they hanged Haman on the gallows he had prepared for Mordecai. Then the king's anger subsided. . . .

On the thirteenth day of Adar, the twelfth month, the time came for the king's command and decree to be carried out. That very day on which the enemies of the Jews had hoped to triumph over them was to become the day when the Jews should triumph over those who hated them. Throughout all the provinces of King Ahasuerus, the Jews assembled in their cities to attack those who had sought to bring disaster on them. None could offer resistance, because fear of them had fallen on all the peoples. The rulers of the princes, the satraps and the governors, and the royal officials all aided the Jews, out of fear of Mordecai. . . .

The rest of the Jews throughout the

king's provinces rallied in self-defence and so had respite from their enemies; they slaughtered seventy-five thousand of those who hated them, but they took no plunder. That was on the thirteenth day of the month of Adar; on the fourteenth day they rested and made it a day of feasting and joy. The Jews in Susa had assembled on both the thirteenth and fourteenth days of the month; they rested on the fifteenth day and made that a day of feasting and joy. This explains why Jews in the countryside who live in remote villages observe the fourteenth day of Adar with joy and feasting as a holiday, sending presents of food to one another.

Mordecai put these things on record, and he sent letters to all the Jews throughout the provinces of King Ahasuerus, both near and far, requiring them to observe annually the fourteenth and fifteenth days of the month of Adar as the days on which the Jews had respite from their enemies; that was the month which was changed for them from sorrow into joy, from a time of mourning to a holiday. They were to observe them as days of feasting and joy, days for sending presents of food to one another and gifts to the poor.

Comments on the Story

The book of Esther, written between the fourth and second centuries B.C.E., addresses the question of Jewish existence in Gentile lands, where life itself could be at risk, compromised by tyrants, or threatened by a competing culture. The book of Esther, which recites the tale of the proposed annihilation of the Jews in Persia and the heroic intervention by Queen Esther, provides a moving paradigm about appropriate Jewish response when threatened by extermination and when challenged by an alternate culture and its values. Esther, the main character, is defined by her society in two ways that lessen her value: She is a woman and a Jew. But within these strictures, she courageously and cleverly acts with independence and strength.

Chapter 7 refers to most of the main characters from the book of Esther: King Ahasuerus, who has chosen Esther from among all the maidens of his kingdom, and does not know she is a Jew; Queen Esther, orphaned as a child and adopted by Mordecai, who advised her that she was the first hope for the Jews' salvation; and Haman, the courtier who ordered the Jews' extermination. The setting is Queen Esther's banquet. Having previously risked her life to approach the king without being summoned, she had him agree to come to her. She withheld the information about the impending doom of the Jews when she twice addressed the king previously; the suspense has built, and now she must act.

Esther has planned her plea intelligently—the perpetrator of the heinous act is also in her presence, for Haman has been invited as well. When the king asks her to state her request, she first reveals the horror of the plan in personal terms; surely the king will sympathize with the most beautiful woman of his realm, now his queen and to whom he has already given a hearing. He stated that he would give her half his kingdom! She begs that her own life and the lives of her people be spared. Ingeniously, she adds that if the decree had only been to sell the Jews into slavery she would not have bothered the king, for that would not have injured his economic interests. Thus Esther has given Ahasuerus two personal reasons to consider the horror of the decree: it would destroy Esther, and it would have severe economic effects. Only after the news has enraged the king does Esther reveal its source: Haman—who is dining with them.

The ingenuity of the plot continues. The king departs to the courtyard in a rage; Haman pleads with Esther for his life. Esther says nothing, but Haman has enraged the king even further because the close position he has taken while speaking to Esther prompts the king to think he is trying to sexually assault her. Thus the evil Haman is made to look as foolish as he has appeared earlier in the text. The man who thought he would be praised by the king had to watch his enemy Mordecai be praised instead. Now the gallows that Haman constructed for Mordecai will be used for him.

With Haman destroyed, the designated day for annihilation of the Jews now is reversed. Innocent Jews are safe and triumph over those who planned to murder them. Even the government officials who were to fight against them must now take orders from Mordecai, who has risen to a position of honor and authority in the king's court. The story, however, does not end without bloodshed. When Haman and his sons are put to death, the killing climaxes, followed by the skirmishes between Jews and the local populace. The attacks against the Jews had begun, and the retaliation is described in terms of self-defense (9:16), stressing that there was no taking of plunder. The story underscores the fact that the cessation of violence and heinous crimes may sometimes only be achieved at the expense of life.

The book of Esther closes with a reference to the celebration of the feast of Purim every year by Jews in the Diaspora. While it may seem strange to some that a holiday based a novella is still observed today, the reversal of fortune is paradigmatic in Jewish experience and for all radical reversals: the Israel that was almost destroyed time and again lives!

Esther's compliance with the king when she is summoned as a member of his harem and her subservience to him and to Mordecai prompts some interpreters to favor the character of the independent Vashti (of the beginning of the book), who refused to obey the king's orders to appear in front of his male guests. Nevertheless, Esther's character is striking. She maximizes every power that she could possibly have within the strictures of her greater society and within the royal court. By being silent about her Jewishness and by pleasing King Ahasuerus sexually, she becomes queen. She took upon herself the risky maneuver of approaching the king before she was summoned, saying only "if I perish, I perish" (4:16). By sagaciously withholding the horrible message to the king, she was able to reveal it while maximizing the potential to hear a favorable response and to free the Jews from their menacing oppressor: Haman.

Retelling the Story

In Shushan, long ago, there lived a foolish king named Ahasuerus, who ruled over 127 provinces from India to Ethiopia. One night in the midst of a great party King Ahasuerus called for his wife to dance before all of the assembled guests. She refused.

The rabbis say that Artaxerxes was the proper name of Ahasuerus (a name that sounds like the Hebrew word for "headache"). Why was he called Ahasuerus rather than his proper name? Because whenever anyone mentioned him, that person's head would hurt. (*Esther Rabbah* 1.3)

"How can a wife refuse to obey her husband?" asked the king's advisers. "If your wife Vashti refuses his Majesty's order, then all of the wives may refuse their husbands all through the kingdom! Your Majesty, you must punish her!"

According to the rabbis, the ultimate humiliation in Ahasuerus's demand that Vashti appear before his guests was that he told her to appear naked. At first she answered the king by attempting to reason with him. She said, "If your guests consider me beautiful, they will want me for themselves and kill you so they might have me. If they do not consider me beautiful, you will be humiliated for having presented me." Apparently, Ahasuerus has a penchant for viewing naked women. Vashti says that as a stable boy in her father's court, Ahasuerus paid prostitutes to parade before him unclothed. Now he was treating her no better than a prostitute. When the king did not answer, the queen reminded him that in her father's court not even those who had committed crimes were stripped of their clothes before being punished. (*Esther Rabbah* 3.13-14)

The foolish king listened to his ministers, and banished his wife from the kingdom. But after a time he became lonely, and decided to take a new queen. The prettiest girls and women of the 127 provinces were brought before the king, that he might choose one who pleased him. And he chose the beautiful Esther.

Now, Esther was an orphan, a Jewish woman in the care of her uncle, Mordecai. When Esther was chosen queen, Mordecai stationed himself at the palace gates to keep close to her. And there Mordecai heard two of the gate-keepers plotting to kill the king. Quickly he informed the king of the plot, and his deed was written in the book of Chronicles.

At this time in Shushan the king's most trusted adviser was named Haman. He was a wicked man, who demanded that all bow down to him. The only one who refused to bow was Esther's uncle, Mordecai. "Why do you disobey the order?" Haman asked. "Because I am a Jew," Mordecai explained, "and I kneel only to God."

This made Haman so angry that he plotted to kill all of the Jews in all of the king's provinces. He cast *pur,* lots, to determine on what day he would have the Jews put to death. The date chosen was the thirteenth day of Adar, the twelfth month. Then Haman told the king, "There is a certain people who do not obey your laws. Let an edict be drawn for their destruction, and I will pay the king's treasury 10,000 talents of silver."

Ahasuerus agreed, and word was sent throughout his kingdom that on the thirteenth of Adar all of the Jews were to be slain.

When the Jews learned of their fate, there was weeping and wailing. Morde-cai put on sackcloth and ashes, and he sent messengers to tell Esther all that had happened. He begged her to ask the king to change his decree.

Now, in those days a queen was not allowed to just go and talk with the king. She had to wait to be summoned, just like everyone else. And if she appeared before the king without being sent for, she risked her life, for if the king did not wish to see her, he could have her killed immediately. But if he held out his scepter to her, he would listen to her request.

Esther told Mordecai that she could not appear before Ahasuerus. "But you must," Mordecai told her, "or all of your people will be killed. And perhaps you, too, will die. You are the only hope for saving the Jewish people."

Esther was afraid. She might lose her life! She fasted and prayed for three days. At last she decided she must go. She approached the king's throne. He looked up at her. Her heart beat wildly. Then he held his scepter out to her. "Your Majesty," she asked, "would you grant me a great favor?" She held her breath.

"Anything you wish, my queen, even if it be to half my kingdom," he replied.

"Would you and your adviser Haman do me the honor of attending a ban-quet with me?"

"Anything you wish," the king replied.

Now, when Haman learned that he had been invited to dine with the king and the queen, he felt even more important and full of himself. As he passed Mordecai at the gate, he was even more angered that Mordecai refused to bow to him. So he hurried home and had constructed a gallows on which he planned to hang Mordecai the next day.

Night fell. The king couldn't sleep. He called for his book of Chronicles. Perhaps some reading would settle his mind. In the annals he found mention that Mordecai the Jew had saved him from an assassination plot.

"How did I thank this Mordecai?" he asked the chamberlain.

"The man was never so honored," came the answer.

"Never honored? Hmmm. . . . Who is about at this hour?"

The chamberlain spotted Haman. "Your adviser Haman, your Majesty."

"Send him to me."

Haman appeared before the king. Ahasuerus asked, "How would you honor a man who has done a great deed for his king?"

Haman thought the king meant to honor him. "I would outfit him in the finest clothes and parade him through the streets on your finest horse," he answered.

"Good," said the king. "Do this for my subject Mordecai."

Haman was furious, though he dared not tell the king. In the morning he paraded Mordecai through the streets, and still his anger grew.

> There were several good things about Ahasuerus, according to the sages. First, he waited three years to become king after he became eligible. Second, he waited four years before he chose a queen and married. Third, he would never take actions without consulting his counselors. Finally, whenever anyone did him a favor, he had it written down. This last attribute saved the lives of many, since Mordecai's good deed had been recorded. (*Esther Rabbah* 1.15)

That day the queen's banquet would be held. Esther wanted to tell the king about Haman's evil plot. She tried, but she couldn't find the words. Her mouth went dry and her hands shook. Instead she asked the king and Haman to attend another feast the next day.

At the second banquet the king asked, "Esther, what is your wish and your request? Even if it be to half the kingdom, it shall be granted."

Esther stood up straight and took a deep breath. "Your Majesty," she began, there is an evil man who wishes to kill me and all my people. Let my life be granted, and grant me the lives of my people. That is my request."

"Who is this evil one?" thundered Ahasuerus.

"There," she pointed, "your adviser, Haman."

The king was furious. He ordered Haman hanged from the gallows built for Mordecai. And Mordecai was made chief adviser to the king.

As for the decree, it could not be changed. But a second decree was issued in which the king allowed the Jews to fight against any who threatened them. On the thirteenth of Adar, there was fighting and bloodshed throughout the kingdom. Perhaps, too, there were places where the people lay down their arms and embraced each other, but of that we do not know.

We do know that when, on the fourteenth of Adar, the Jewish people were still alive, there was feasting and joy. And to this day the festival of Purim commemorates the foolish Ahasuerus, the wise Mordecai, the evil Haman, and the beautiful Esther, who with her bravery helped to save her people. *(Betty Lehrman)*

The archangel Michael was the defense attorney for the Jewish people before God, the judge of all. Haman, as prosecutor, leveled charge after charge against the Jews. Michael answered every one of these charges. In his summation, Michael contended that all the Jews were guilty of was refusing to bow to idols or shed blood. Their only crime had been keeping God's laws. Hearing this, the one who judges all hearts reaffirmed the divine covenant never to forsake the Jewish people. (*Esther Rabbah* 7.12)

Esther

A later midrash on the Esther story, written in Greek, that portrays God's role in the story.

The Story

On the third day, after ending her prayers, Esther put off the clothes she had worn while she worshipped, and arrayed herself in her robes of state. When she was attired in all her splendour and had invoked the all-seeing God, her preserver, she took her two maids with her; on one she leaned for support, as befitted a fine lady, while the other followed, bearing her train. She was radiant and in the height of her beauty; her face was as cheerful as it was lovely, but her heart was constricted with fear. She passed through all the doors until she stood in the royal presence. The king was seated on his throne in the full array of his majesty, all gold and precious stones, an awe-inspiring figure. He looked up, his face aglow with regal dignity, and regarded her with towering anger. The queen sank down, changing colour and fainting, and she swooned on the shoulder of the maid who went before her.

But the king's mood was changed by God to one of gentleness. In deep concern he started up from his throne and held her in his arms until she came to herself. He soothed her with reassuring words: 'Esther, what is it? Have no fear of me, your loving husband; you shall not die, for our order is only for our subjects. You may approach.' The king raised his gold sceptre and touched her neck; then he kissed her and said, 'You may speak to me.' She answered, 'My lord, I saw you like an angel of God; I was awestruck at your glorious appearance. Your countenance is so full of grace, my lord, that I look in wonder.' But while she was speaking she sank down fainting; the king was distressed, and his attendants all tried to reassure her. . . .

Mardochaeus [Mordecai] said, 'This is God's doing, for I have been reminded of the dream I had about these matters; every one of the visions I saw his been fulfilled. There was the little spring which became a river, and there was light and sun and abundant water: the river is Esther, whom the king married and made queen; the two dragons are Haman and myself; the nations are those who combined to blot out all memory of the Jews; my nation is Israel, which cried out to God and was delivered. The Lord has delivered his people, he has rescued us from all these evils. God performed great signs and portents, such as have never occurred among the nations. He prepared two lots, one for the people of God and one for all the nations; then came the hour and the time for these two lots to be cast, the judgment by God upon all the nations; he remembered his people and gave the verdict for his heritage.

So they are to keep these days in the month of Adar, the fourteenth and fifteenth of that month, by assembling with joy and gladness before God from one generation of his people Israel to another for ever.'

Comments on the Story

The absence of direct reference to God or use of God's name in the book of Esther and the uncertainty in antiquity of the legitimacy of celebrating Purim are the most likely reasons for the debate over its inclusion in the canon. Apparently, it was not considered part of Scripture in the Qumran community, which gave us the Dead Sea Scrolls, because not only were no copies or portions of the book found there, but also because the holiday of Purim was not included in any calendars of religious celebrations. Its canonicity was debated by Jews into the third and fourth centuries C.E. and by Eastern Christians into the seventh century. The additions to Esther, composed *circa* the second century B.C.E., are replete with references to God (unlike the book proper), and change the tone of the book from highlighting the practical wisdom and courage of Esther and Mordecai in confronting peril to emphasizing divine intervention in times of threat. Esther 15:1-16 emphasizes God's control over King Ahasuerus's decision to spare Esther's life, and Esther 10:4-13 details Mordecai's realization that his dream was a message from God, who is faithful to the inheritance of the Jews.

Esther 15:1-16. In the Hebrew Masoretic text, the description of Esther's fear of approaching the king unsummoned and the king's response to her when she does arrive are described briefly and without delayed suspense. In this addition, however, great care is made to capitalize on the most personally suspenseful part of the work. Would Esther lose her life due to the enraged king? Esther's own anxiety is underscored; not only does her calm demeanor belie her anguished soul, but also she "faltered, and turned pale and faint" (v. 7) when she saw the king. In the Masoretic text, she fasted in preparation of her visit, but in the addition she fasts and prays (14:1-19). In this section she also maximizes her changes for a favorable response by dressing in her most resplendent attire, capitalizing on her position as queen and recalling the beginning of the story when King Ahasuerus chose her from among all women of the region.

This addition continues to add to the suspense of the narrative by describing the king. He is removed from Esther in temperament and authority as well as in physical distance; she must go "through all the doors" (v. 6) to reach him. He is described in the royal posture and is indeed "terrifying" to behold. The reader understands Esther's terrible situation by the description

162

of the king's face—it is filled with anger. By the time Esther faints, there does not appear to be much hope; the queen cannot even speak. But precisely at this climactic moment, God intervenes, changing the king's emotions and filling him with kindness. In effusive gestures, the king comes to care for Esther. He picks her up until she regains consciousness and speaks gently to her, reassuring her three times that she will not die. He not only states so directly, but also says that the law does not apply to her; he holds out the golden scepter and reassures her that she may speak. The tremendous tension that has been built up by additions C and D is resolved because of God's direct participation. Even Esther, however, has not fully recovered. She states that the king's appearance was as frightening as an angel of God, and she faints again. As another example of God's hand in changing the king's character, he is disturbed by Esther's fainting, another sign of his concern for her. The text that follows at this point is from the book of Esther proper, and it continues with Esther's formal request for Ahasuerus and Haman to attend her feast.

10:4-13. In this section, the final addition to Esther completes the first (11:1-12, Addition A), wherein Mordecai recognized that he had a dream from God and sought its understanding. Mordecai now understands the salvation that his people have received in terms of apocalyptic imagery. As in the book of Daniel, in this type of genre, dragons or beasts typically are used to represent nations that threaten to destroy the Jews. By incorporating this apocalyptic addition, the book of Esther presents a more fearful attitude toward foreign nations, and probably reflects the more difficult and threatening period the Jews experienced in the Hellenistic age.

Some commentators have suggested that the additions, which portray an intervening God, detract from the resourcefulness of humans (Mordecai, Esther) in resolving the threats to the Jews and the problems of living in a Gentile world. But the portrayal is not one where humans are passive and simply wait for the intervention of God. The additions also emphasize the importance of being faithful to Jewish customs (prayer, *kashrut)* as well as reliance on God. The importance of human action is not lost in the additions. Thus, given that the additions do not *replace* the canonical text, it may be possible that their author was simply trying to add another theological dimension. In addition D, for example, Esther takes responsibility for dressing as royalty in order to increase her chances of receiving a hearing from the king. Thus, even with the additions to the book, Esther still receives credit for her actions and courage.

Retelling the Story

We've heard of Esther's bravery, how through her God saved her people. But what must it have felt like to confront the king? To go to his throne room

163

unbidden, not knowing if he would receive her, or if her life would be taken from her?

Queen Esther usually lived in the company of women. In the morning her maids would awaken her and rub her skin with sweet oils, that it would always be soft. They brought fragrant teas for her to drink and cakes to eat, so that her mouth always smelled sweet and her stomach was pleasantly full. She spent her days walking in the garden, smelling the flowers. She visited with the other women of the court. She watched the sun rise and set and the days grow longer and then shorter again.

> The rabbis say that after Ahasuerus had executed Vashti for refusing to appear before his guests, he had second thoughts. After her death the king began to regret his decision. Too late he finally saw that Vashti had been right to refuse a request that was inappropriate in the first place. (*Esther Rabbah* 5.2)

Whenever Ahasuerus the king sent for her, Esther's maids dressed her quickly and skillfully, and she answered his summons willingly. For long hours she listened to stories and answered his queries, reading his moods and taking care with her responses. She had never felt free to speak her own mind; he was the king, and she knew she was merely queen for his pleasure.

Now she must broach this difficult subject. His favorite counselor, his most trusted adviser, was planning to destroy her people. And Ahasuerus had already signed the decree authorizing the destruction!

At first she thought it wasn't possible. For so long she had served others, taking care of Mordecai, and then tending to the king's desires. How could she even tell Ahasuerus what he had done? Mordecai insisted she tell the king, and she knew he was right. No one else could save her people. She alone had the king's ear—or did she? The thoughts nagged at her as she fasted and prayed and took more than usual care with her morning and evening ablutions. At last the three days of prayer and fasting were over. It was time to go to Ahasuerus. She was the hope of her people. She must try to speak to him, even if it cost her life.

Esther arrayed herself in her finest garments. She took her two most trusted maids, holding on to the arm of one while the other carried her train. She hoped she looked as lovely as the day Ahasuerus had chosen her to be his bride. The fear in her heart rose to her face as a red flush. She looked radiant.

Esther and the maids passed through the corridors of the castle until at last they came to the throne room. There was the king. The sunlight shone on his face, and his bejeweled cape gleamed. The lights danced in Esther's eyes as she peered at his golden scepter. If he would just look at her and smile—if he would just raise the scepter and beckon to her.

Ahasuerus lifted his face. It was flushed with fierce anger. Esther felt her own face grow pale, and she faltered, lost her balance, and collapsed in a faint against her maid.

The guards stepped forward, ready to seize the queen. At that moment God reminded Ahasuerus of his love for this frail, beautiful woman. The king sprang from his throne and gathered her into his arms, searching her face. "What is it, Esther? What's wrong, my love? I am your husband. Take care, you shall not die, for our law applies only to our subjects. Do not be afraid."

The king lifted his bride and gently brought her to her feet. Then he raised the golden scepter and gently touched her with it. He caressed her shoulder. "Come near. Speak to me, my love."

Esther tried to speak her mind, to tell him of her plight. But her heart was filled only with the thought that she would not die. The words would not come to her lips. How could she tell him? "I know . . . Your servant. . . . " Again she fainted and fell.

Now the king was truly concerned. He called for water and wine. The servants rushed to do his bidding, to restore her. Finally she regained her breath. She sat on a golden stool and sipped from a jeweled chalice. At first she didn't trust herself to speak, but gradually the wine warmed her and the color returned to her cheeks. When her breath grew strong and she knew her voice was sure, she asked, "Your Majesty, would you grant me a great favor?"

"Anything you wish, my queen, even if it to be half my kingdom," he replied.

She could not tell him then. She needed to be alone with him, to make sure he was in a receptive mood, that he wouldn't lose his temper—or worse yet, laugh at her people's tragedy. "Would you and your adviser Haman do me the honor of attending a banquet with me?"

"Anything you wish," came the answer.

She smiled and bowed her head. She would fill him with his favorite foods and delightful conversation, and then tell him of the murderous decree. And

> Usually a eunuch was placed in charge of the women of a king's court. The sages suggest that Haman was impotent, and that was the only reason he was allowed to have anything to do with the women of the king's court. (*Esther Rabbah* 5.3)

perhaps he would listen. Perhaps her people could be saved. She resolved that she, Esther, would have the courage to tell Ahasuerus all that had been done. *(Betty Lehrman)*

Mordecai's Dream

"Mordecai, what's the matter?" Joshua asked the old man as he walked into the hall. It was their weekly meeting, when Mordecai and his closest friends met to ponder the problems of the kingdom and share the joys of the day.

> Haman had three hundred sixty-five advisers, one for each day of the year. But none of them offered the quality of advice given him by his wife, Zeresh. She told her husband that if he wanted to get the better of Mordecai, Haman would have to come up with a punishment that had not already been devised by the God of the Jews. After all, these people had survived the wilderness, the fiery furnace, the lion's den, and the pit. Hearing this, Haman decided to have a gallows built so that Mordecai could be hanged. Then he stood on it to show the executioner how he was to do away with this troublesome Jew. Little did Haman know. . . . (*Esther Rabbah* 9.2)

Mordecai sat on his accustomed stool. "I had a dream," he said, shaking his head from side to side. "I had a dream."

"So, tell your friends what you dreamt, we'll figure out what it means." The men gathered around, eager to hear the dream. Was it prophecy? Prediction? Good news? Or bad?

"It was long ago," Mordecai began. "I just remembered it. I didn't know then what it meant."

"Tell us," urged a man named Simeon. "Tell us everything you remember."

"I saw . . . there was a rushing stream." Mordecai closed his eyes, concentrating. "It sparkled until it became a wild torrent, a river. And the sunlight danced off the water, lots of water. Then two dragons came and did battle by the river. The river healed the wounds of one dragon and drowned the other. And there were many nations, and one cried out to God."

"Two dragons? Why two dragons? Are the dragons men, fighting each other?" Joshua jumped in.

"No, no, the dragons are armies," Simeon insisted.

"Perhaps the dragons are two sides of an issue—two opinions doing battle," said another.

"And a stream becoming a river," said another man. "Surely we are discussing the power of a great man, growing."

"The stream is the nation of Israel growing stronger." Simeon was growing more excited.

"And the nations?" asked Joshua. "What about the nations?"

Mordecai listened to the debates, the arguments. Finally he stood and announced. "I know the meaning of the dream." All of the men stopped talking about it and looked at their leader. "The river is Esther, the queen, who grew from a small stream to a powerful torrent, full of light and beauty. The two dragons who did battle are myself and Haman. And the nations are those that gathered to destroy the name of the Jews."

"But the one nation?" asked Simeon.

"That is clear," answered Mordecai quietly. "The one nation which cried out to God is Israel. And God heard our cry and has rescued us."

"But what is the significance of the dream?" Joshua leaned closer, his brow furrowed.

"God has given us great signs and wonders," Mordecai continued. "For the stream to become a torrent . . . for the dragons to do battle and the good dragon to win . . . for our nation's cries to be heard . . . God remembered the people of Israel, and we must remember this deliverance. Every year, on the fourteenth and fifteenth days of the month of Adar, we must celebrate with joy and gladness, from generation to generation, forever."

> The sages say the reason Ahasuerus could not sleep on the night he was reminded of Mordecai's good deed toward him was that he had been awakened by a terrifying dream. The king had dreamed that Haman had attempted to assassinate him. Shaken by what he dreamed, the king asked his servant to read to him and heard of another attempt on his life, one that had been thwarted by Mordecai. (*Esther Rabbah* 10.1)

"Ah, of course. We must teach our children and their children and their children's children. We must remember," Joshua intoned.

"Yes," repeated the others, "we must remember." *(Betty Lehrman)*

The Virtuous Woman

In the proverbs, both virtue and wisdom are personified by a female figure.

The Story

Wisdom cries aloud in the open air, and raises her voice in public places.
She calls at the top of the bustling streets;
at the approaches to the city gates she says:
'How long will you simple fools be content with your simplicity?
If only you would respond to my reproof,
I would fill you with my spirit and make my precepts known to you.
But because you refused to listen to my call,
because no one heeded when I stretched out my hand,
because you rejected all my advice and would have none of my reproof,
I in turn shall laugh at your doom and deride you when terror comes,
when terror comes like a hurricane and your doom approaches like a whirlwind,
when anguish and distress come upon you. . . .

Hear how wisdom calls and understanding lifts her voice.
She takes her stand at the crossroads,
by the wayside, at the top of the hill; beside the gate, at the entrance to the city,
at the approach by the portals she cried aloud:
'It is to you I call,
to all mankind I appeal . . .

Who can find a good wife?
Her worth is far beyond red coral.
Her husband's whole trust is in her, and children are not lacking.
She works to bring him good, not evil,
all the days of her life.
She chooses wool and flax
and with a will she sets about her work.
Like a ship laden with merchandise she brings home food from far off.
She rises while it is still dark
and apportions food for her household,
with a due share for her servants.
After careful thought she buys a field and plants a vineyard out of her earnings.
She sets about her duties resolutely and tackles her work with vigour.
She sees that her business goes well, and all night long her lamp does not go out.

169

She holds the distaff in her hand,
and her fingers grasp the spindle.
She is open-handed to the wretched
and extends help to the poor.
When it snows she has no fear for
her household,
for they are wrapped in double
cloaks.
She makes her own bed coverings
and clothing of fine linen and purple.
Her husband is well known in the
assembly,
where he takes his seat with the
elders of the region.
She weaves linen and sells it,
and supplies merchants with sashes.
She is clothed in strength and dignity
and can afford to laugh at tomorrow.
When she opens her mouth, it is to
speak wisely;

her teaching is sound.
She keeps her eye on the conduct of
her household
and does not eat the bread of idleness.
Her sons with one accord extol her
virtues;
her husband too is loud in her
praise;
'Many a woman shows how gifted
she is;
but you excel them all.'
Charm is deceptive and beauty
fleeting;
but the woman who fears the LORD is
honoured.
Praise her for all she has
accomplished;
let her achievements bring her
honor at the city gates.

Comments on the Story

The book of Proverbs, a collection of wisdom sayings, consists of a collection of materials from Israel, some dating back to the monarchic period but edited in the post-exilic era. Its instructional voice shows that it comes from bureaucrats and educators, although some aphorisms appear to derive from folk wisdom. A comparison with literature from Egypt and Mesopotamia shows ancient Near Eastern influences. Wisdom literature focuses on insight that is gained from knowledge of God's creation, from experience, and from observation. In the Hebrew Bible, God's revelation is often seen in the covenant and its teachings (or laws), in Israel's history, and in God's creation. It is this later aspect that is stressed in wisdom literature, although sometimes features of the covenant and Israel's history are included as well. Throughout the book of Proverbs, female imagery features prominently. The beginning of the collection shows Wisdom itself personified as a magnificent woman. The book ends with a description of the woman of valor—a woman whose many virtues are extolled. The texts selected here portray Woman Wisdom and the woman of valor positively, yet the entirety of the book of Proverbs also caricatures women as the temptresses who lead innocent men astray. Given that these texts arise from a society where women's voices could only be derivative of men's, it is not surprising that women are portrayed stereotypically: either on a pedestal or debased.

170

Proverbs 1:20-33; 8:1-4, 22-31. Chapters 1–8 of Proverbs, like much of the book, are written in poetic parallelism, wherein the second line of each couplet repeats or extends the idea of the first line. Wisdom is personified as a woman. Like the prophets and messengers of God who encounter persons in the busy city center, so too does Wisdom speak in public places, streets, and at the city gates, the place where judicial decisions were often rendered. Wisdom is not restricted to the elite, nor is it hidden from the general population. All one has to do to acquire it is simply to seek it. The search for wisdom, moreover, is aided by Wisdom itself: Wisdom beckons. When its call is not heeded, Wisdom goes further—it admonishes those who have shunned it, saying "Give heed to my reproof" (1:23). Wisdom, however, who so persistently calls to her audience, is not infinitely patient. One's acceptance or rejection of her offerings will have consequences.

Wisdom, or the spurning of it, is also portrayed as responsible for the lot of people in life. Proverbs 1:32-33 presents a simplistic world view where those who follow Wisdom and knowledge are rewarded with an untroubled life, whereas those who reject its teachings find misery. Proverbs 8:35-36 states its terms more starkly. Those who follow wisdom have life, whereas those who reject her "are in love with death."

Although the characteristics of wisdom are not delineated in these sections, wisdom is associated with knowledge (1:29), which is in poetic parallelism with "fear of the LORD." Thus Wisdom's association with God is made clear from the beginning of the book. Proverbs 8:22-31 speaks about the origins of wisdom itself. Just as a description of the origins of humankind or the origins of Israel tell us about the essence of these things or give insight into what people value about creation and Israel, so too does the description of Wisdom's origin tell us about the nature of wisdom itself. In other words, the account is not to be read literally but poetically, as is the writing itself. Wisdom was created by God, before other things of the universe were made (8:22). This theology emphasizes that not only are tangible things created by God, but so too are some of the most treasured, intangible human values, such as wisdom and knowledge. To treasure wisdom is to value God and God's teachings, for wisdom was God's "darling and delight" (8:30). Just as Wisdom sought its hearers in chapter 1, so too did Wisdom, when first created (8:31), take joy in humankind.

Proverbs 31:10-31. As the book of Proverbs opens with female imagery, so too does it end with the idealization of the virtuous woman/wife (in Hebrew, the words for "woman" and "wife" are the same, although in this instance "wife" is more appropriate because of the references to husband and sons). The woman complies with patriarchal values: She runs an orderly household, provides free labor and organizational skills, exercises financial knowledge for the good of the family, and ensures that her sons conduct themselves properly.

Nevertheless, in this restricted context, she is praised for her justice as well. She cares for the servants and the poor.

In spite of the stereotyped view in Proverbs of women as strangers and temptresses, it is remarkable that Proverbs includes more positive portrayals of women. The image of Wisdom as a personified woman challenged its past audience and continues to remind audiences today to consider women as more than the servants or temptresses of men. It also prompts readers to consider the feminine dimension of the transcendent. The book's conclusion with the woman of virtue, however, points to a more subtle stereotyping. If women can only be praised as men's servants, is this really praise? Perhaps in an ancient community it was the best one could expect, but its transparency challenges the modern reader and storyteller to imagine better.

Retelling the Story

There was once a king who had three daughters. As he was getting older, the king wanted to divide his kingdom among them, but he didn't know which princess should rule after him upon his death. So he sent them all out into the world, to prove themselves worthy of the crown.

The first daughter traveled to many distant kingdoms. Everywhere tales of her beauty preceded her, and everywhere she was met with rich presents. She had a knack for business, and shrewdly bought and sold many things. She returned home a wealthy woman with beautiful possessions.

> Some of the rabbis say that the virtuous woman of the proverbs is the Torah herself. The Torah personified as a woman is God's companion from before the beginning of creation. (*Genesis Rabbah* 8.2)

The second daughter studied many arts, until she mastered the secret of spinning the most wondrous cloths. She spun fabric that looked as if it were made of snowflakes, clothes that looked seamed of moonbeams, tapestries that gleamed from within, as if from sunlight. She, too, returned home a rich woman.

The third daughter began her travels uncertain of where her destiny lay. She read many books and maps and studied the languages and the law of the land. For months she journeyed, listening and learning until she understood all the peoples of her father's kingdom. At last she returned home. There she sought counsel of her closest friend, a young man who loved learning just as much as she. They talked and talked for many days and nights, until they realized they were deeply in love. With the blessings of the king, the princess and the young man were soon married.

When it came time for the king to divide his kingdom, he gave one third of his wealth to his eldest daughter, for she knew how to manage riches. To the second daughter he also gave one third, for her skill had taught her to appreciate fine things.

But it was to the third princess that he gave his crown and lands, for she understood the peoples of his kingdom, both near and far. And a kingdom must be ruled with wisdom and love.

The princess became queen, and her husband became king. Together they ruled wisely and well for many, many years. *(Betty Lehrman)*

Wisdom is attained little by little, according to the sages. A fool looks at a huge hill and says, "I could never move that." But a wise person looks at the same hill and says, "I could move a basketload of dirt today and another tomorrow." Just so, the fool thinks that Torah is too much to learn, while a wise person studies day by day and verse by verse. Likewise, someone foolish entering a kitchen looks at a loaf of bread hanging out of reach and says, "I could never reach that high." But a wise person assumes that if someone could put the bread up there, someone else can get it down. So she gets a stool and gets the bread. Just so, a fool says, "The Torah is too lofty for me to understand" and gives up. But a wise person climbs step by step to reach the heights of the Torah. (*Leviticus Rabbah* 19.2)

Gomer

Gomer, an unchaste woman, is chosen as Hosea's wife only to make a statement about the relationship between God and Israel.

The Story

The word of the Lord which came to Hosea son of Beeri during the reigns of Uzziah, Jotham, Ahaz, and Hezekiah, kings of Judah, and during the reign of Jeroboam son of Joash king of Israel.

This is the beginning of the LORD's message given by Hosea. He said, 'Go and take an unchaste woman as your wife, and with the woman have children; for like an unchaste woman this land is guilty of unfaithfulness to the LORD.' So he married Gomer daughter of Diblaim, and she conceived and bore him a son. The LORD said to Hosea, 'Call him Jezreel, for in a little while I am going to punish the dynasty of Jehu for the blood shed in the valley of Jezreel, and bring the kingdom of Israel to an end. On that day I shall break Israel's bow in the vale of Jezreel.' Gomer conceived again and bore a daughter, and the LORD said to Hosea,
Call her Lo-ruhamah;
for I shall never again show love to
    Israel,
never again forgive them.

But Judah I shall love and save.
I shall save them not by bow or
    sword or weapon of war,
not by horses and horsemen,
but I shall save them by the LORD
    their God.
After weaning Lo-ruhamah, Gomer conceived and bore a son; and the LORD said,
Call him Lo-ammi;
for you are not my people,
and I shall not be your God.
The Israelites will be as countless as
    the sands of the sea,
which can neither be measured nor
    numbered;
it will no longer be said to them,
    'You are not my people';
they will be called Children of the
    Living God.
The people of Judah and of Israel will
    be united
and will choose for themselves one
    leader;
they will spring up from the land,
for great will be the day of Jezreel.

Comments on the Story

Although not much is known about the prophet Hosea, it is clear from his preaching that he addressed the community of Israel (the Northern Kingdom) from the decades of its prosperity in the mid-eighth century until shortly before its decline and fall to Assyria in 721 B.C.E. The first chapter of Hosea introduces Gomer, the promiscuous woman whom God told Hosea to marry, as a symbol of the wayward Israel. The relationship of Gomer and Hosea represents the entirety of the experience of God with Israel: past, present, and future. It is one filled with unfaithfulness but also with hope.

Gomer's origin and character are hidden. The name of her father is given, but nothing is known about Diblaim. Sometimes Gomer is identified as a prostitute, but this is an unfair translation of the Hebrew *eshet-zenunim* (v. 2). The phrase, which literally means "woman of fornication," translates *not* into harlot, but rather "unfaithful woman," "promiscuous woman," "unchaste woman," or the like. The importance of Gomer in this text is as metaphor. The use of poetry to describe her actions, her children, her punishment, and her restoration is appropriate because the author's point is that Gomer is unfaithful to Hosea just as Israel is unfaithful to God. It is Israel's relationship with God that is the true issue of the book of Hosea. Nevertheless, sexual imagery is appropriate in so far as it relates to Israel's interest in Canaanite religion and its infatuation with the fertility cult of Baal.

Unfortunately, Gomer and the sexual symbolism used to describe her can be misunderstood and unfairly applied to women today in a way that stereotypes them as temptresses and adulteresses who need to be shunned or punished. Clearly the text comes from a society in which women's sexuality was controlled by patriarchal structures. Women were seen to be more culpable for adulterous liaisons than men. Both men and women participated at times in the cultic sexual practices of Baal, but in this case the emphasis is on the unfaithful woman. Although the book of Hosea also includes the metaphor of Israel as an unfaithful son and God as the patient and loving adoptive parent (Hosea 11), the image of the prophet Hosea and his unchaste wife dominates, both in opening and in closing the book.

Hosea is told that he will have children from this unchaste woman, just as Israel must bear the fruit of its sinful ways. The names of the children are symbolic of the judgment passed on Israel, and with the birth of each one a harsher sentence is imposed. The first son is named Jezreel, indicating the punishment that is coming for the political crimes of the Northern Kingdom. Jezreel, a battlefield in the Northern Kingdom, was the site of the destruction of the Omri dynasty by the usurper Jehu. Although the Omri dynasty was also marked by unfaithfulness, this text shows that Jehu and his successors initiated their reign by murder and continued heinous acts. The sentence is ominous; God says the dynasty of Israel will end and Israel's military strength will cease.

The second child will be called Lo-ruhamah, meaning "not pitied." The pity and love that God says will no longer be given to Israel are not only emotional or tender qualities but they signify covenantal fidelity as well. The thrust is powerful—twice it is indicated that God will "never again" (v. 6) love or forgive Israel. The extent of God's punishment, however, is immediately tempered by the delineation of its limits. God's love and protection will still extend to Judah, the Southern Kingdom.

The third child is to be named Lo-ammi, or "not my people." Echoing the punishment indicated by the naming of Lo-ruhamah, God specifies that not only will the nation no longer receive God's love and pity—punishments that Israel has endured in the past—but that they are also no longer God's people. In words that echo the formation of the covenant at Sinai, God negates the covenant: "You are not my people, and I shall not be your God" (v. 8).

The theme of Hosea's marriage to Gomer and the importance of the names of the children continue throughout the book. The sins of Israel are lamented. Israel has looked to Baal for sustenance and did not know that it was God who provided for them, just as Gomer did not recognize the care and protection of her husband. Hosea will expose the shame of Gomer's nakedness, just as God will expose that of Israel. The covenant in all its implication has been broken; there are sins of dishonesty, robbery, murder, and the abandonment of justice.

In spite of the harshness of the metaphor, chapter 1 quickly points to the future relationship that Israel will enjoy with God, and the book of Hosea also ends with the hope for the future love and support God will give to a flourishing Israel. Just as the children were given names to symbolize Israel's punishment, so too will they be given new names, or their names will take on new meanings. Thus Jezreel will symbolize the future victory that a united Israel (Israel and Judah) will have over its oppressors. "Not my people" and "Not loved" will no longer characterize the people that God again will have as the "Children of the living God" (v. 10) who "are loved" (2:1). God's retreat from Israel and the covenant will actually accomplish the intentions of the covenant: once again God and people will be united in love and fidelity.

The image of Gomer is distasteful and makes many people today uncomfortable. Not only is she caricatured as a woman with unrestrained lust, but her punishment (described in chapter 2) is filled with violence and shame. Feminists try to prod society into recognizing the frequent powerlessness of women when politics and social welfare are determined mostly by men, and where violence perpetrated against women is commonplace. An image of a promiscuous woman being reprimanded by a righteous man, sanctioned by God, could easily be abused. This reading reminds us that the social origins of a biblical text must be considered when applying it to present concerns.

Retelling the Story

Dear Hosea:

You were the one who said, "I knew what you were when I married you." And that is true. I was no virgin; you knew that. You knew "what" you were getting in our marriage, but I had no idea what I was getting into. The problem is that we never got to know "who" we were married to.

We have been characters in a little play written by your God. You were cast as the God figure, the good husband, and I as the unfaithful wife. We have each played our parts as expected. Had I repented, had I been good, God's little scenario would have been ruined. You and your God depended on my unfaithfulness, and I failed neither of you. You might say I was faithful to the role in which I was cast.

Each of our children became a character in our morality play. They could not be named as other children. We could not draw from the rich pool of family names nor the flowing stream of names from the ancient people of faith. No, our children must serve as symbols of something more in this drama. Jezreel, our first, was named for the valley of both crime and punishment. But his case is not the worst.

The sages compare God's love for Israel to a king who becomes angry with his queen. The king was heard to say, "She is not my wife and her children are not my children." But strangely enough he went directly to the marketplace and spoke with a jeweler about making her a necklace and ring. When others heard of his actions, they were very confused. Why would he say she is no longer his wife and then go have jewelry made for her? The rabbis say that the same uncanny logic applies to God, who had Gomer's children named Lo-ruhamah ("Not loved") and Lo-ammi ("Not my people"), but never deserted the people entirely. (*Numbers Rabbah* 2.15)

There is Lo-ruhamah, our daughter. Have you ever asked yourself what it does to a child to be named Not Loved? Would you expect a child you named Dullard to be wise? Or one named Meanness to be kind? Did you ever consider how she would be regarded when she came to an age for marriage with a name like Not Loved? Must one girl child carry all the punishment for a nation's guilt?

Then our son Lo-ammi arrived, to be greeted with the name Not My People. Is it any surprise that he considered himself disowned at birth with such a name? Call me what you will, but these children have done nothing to deserve humiliating names that serve only as reminders of a guilt that is not truly theirs. Each time they are called, they are condemned.

I am not asking that you and your God completely rewrite the script. All I want is to know that justice is being done, that the punishment suits the crime. If the nation has sinned, let the nation be punished. If I have sinned, let me be punished. But do not afflict the innocent along with the guilty. And cease playing out your scenes of retribution with my children. They are mine, you know. You often doubted that they were yours, but there was never any doubt that they are mine. I have the memory of blood and pain as proof.

So now I end this letter. Why I began it, I do not know, except in the hope that perhaps my side of our story would not go unspoken. Yes, you knew "what" I was—a thing, not a human, another symbol in your revengeful little allegory. You married, not Gomer, but the unfaithful wife, and I have kept faith with you in that. You have been able to be righteous, even compassionate, only because I was willing to play my role. So I have not been faithless in everything. You have kept your honor and good name through my faithful unfaithfulness. Now how will you and your God regard such service?

> The rabbis tell another story about God's relationship with Israel. They say that God is like a scholar who sent his son to school, but the son went instead and played with some companions. When the father found out that his son had played hooky, he disciplined him. But that evening the father invited his son to dinner. Such is the shortness of God's anger and the length of God's love for Israel. (*Numbers Rabbah* 2.15)

Gomer
(Michael E. Williams)

179

Susanna

Susanna is falsely accused of adultery by two religious leaders but is later vindicated.

The Story

No one else was there apart from the two elders, who had hidden and were spying on her. She said to the maids, 'Bring me olive oil and unguents, and shut the garden doors so that I may bathe.' They did as she said: they made fast the garden doors and went out by the side entrance for the things they had been told to bring; they did not see the elders, because they were in hiding.

As soon as the maids had gone, the two elders got up and ran to Susanna. 'Look, the garden doors are shut,' they said, 'and no one can see us! We are overcome with desire for you; consent, and yield to us. If you refuse, we shall swear in evidence there was a young man with you and that was why you sent your maids away.' Susanna groaned and said: 'It is a desperate plight I am in! If I do this, the penalty is death; if I do not, you will have me at your mercy. My choice is made: I will not do it! Better to be at your mercy than to sin against the LORD!' With that she called out at the top of her voice, but the two elders shouted her down, and one of them ran and opened the garden door. The household, hearing the uproar in the garden, rushed in through the side entrance to see what had happened to her. When the elders had told their story, the servants were deeply shocked, but no such allegation had ever been made against Susanna.

Next day, when the people gathered at her husband Joakim's house, the two elders arrived, intent on their criminal design to have Susanna put to death. In the presence of the people they said, 'Send for Susanna daughter of Hilkiah, Joakim's wife.' She was summoned, and came with her parents and children and all her relatives. Now Susanna was a woman of great beauty and delicate feeling. She was closely veiled, but those scoundrels ordered her to be unveiled so that they might feast their eyes on her beauty. Her family and all who saw her were in tears.

Then the two elders stood up before the people and put their hands on her head, she meanwhile looking towards heaven through her tears, for her trust was in the LORD. The elders said: 'As we were walking by ourselves in the garden, this woman came in with her two maids. She shut the garden doors and dismissed her maids, and then a young man, who had been in hiding, came and lay with her. We were in a corner of the garden, and when we saw this wicked-ness we ran towards them. We saw them in the act, but we could not hold the man; he was too strong for us' he opened the door and got clean away. We seized the woman and asked who the young man was, but she would not tell us. That is our evidence.'

Because they were elders of the peo-ple and judges, the assembly believed them and condemned her to death. Then raising her voice Susanna cried: 'Eternal God, you know all secrets and foresee all things, you know that their evidence against me is false. And now I am to die, innocent though I am of the charges these wicked men have brought against me.'

The LORD heard her cry, and as she was being led off to execution, God inspired a devout young man named Daniel to protest. He shouted out, 'I will not have this woman's blood on my hands.' At this the people all turned towards him and demanded, 'What do you mean?' He stepped forward and said: 'Are you such fools, you Israelites, as to condemn a woman of Israel, with-out making careful enquiry and finding out the truth? Reopen the trial; the evi-dence these men have given against her is false.'

Everyone hurried back, and the rest of the elders said to Daniel, 'Come, take your place among us and state your case, for God has given you the standing of an elder.' He said, 'Sepa-rate these men and keep them at a dis-tance from each other, and I shall examine them.' When they had been separated, Daniel summoned one of them. 'You hardened reprobate,' he began, 'the sins of your past have now come home to you. You have given unjust decisions, condemning the inno-cent and acquitting the guilty, although

the LORD has said, "You must not cause the death of the innocent and guilt-less." Now, if you really saw this woman, then tell us, under what tree did you see them together?' He answered, 'Under a clove tree.' Daniel retorted, 'Very good! This lie has cost you your life, for already God's angel has received your sentence from God, and he will cleave you in two.' He ordered him to stand aside, and told them to bring forward the other.

He said to him: 'Spawn of Canaan, no son of Judah, beauty has been your undoing and lust has perverted your heart! So this is how the two of you have been treating the women of Israel, terrifying them into yielding to you! But here is a woman of Judah who would not submit to your villainy. Now tell me, under what tree did you surprise them together?' 'Under a yew tree,' he replied. Daniel said to him, 'Very good! This lie has cost you also your life, for the angel of God is waiting sword in hand to hew you down and destroy the pair of you.'

At that the whole assembly shouted aloud, praising God, the Saviour of those who trust in him. They turned on the two elders, for out of their own mouths Daniel had convicted them of giving false evidence; they dealt with them according to the law of Moses, putting them to death as they in their wickedness had intended to do to their neighbour. So as innocent life was saved that day. Then Hilkiah and his wife gave praise for their daughter Susanna, as did also her husband Joakim and all her relatives, because she was found innocent of a shameful deed.

From that day forward Daniel was held in great esteem among the people.

Comments on the Story

The story of Susanna, included in the apocryphal additions to Daniel, may well have circulated independently of Daniel, given its setting in a relatively autonomous Jewish community at Babylon (as opposed to King Nebuchadnezzar's court in Daniel) and its inclusion of Daniel only at the end of the account. Susanna figures prominently throughout this narrative, which stands on its own in plot and theme. The story of an innocent woman trapped by lecherous, corrupt officials, it highlights the holiness of the Torah of Moses. Although the wicked may try to subvert the Torah, the truly righteous will follow it, even unto death. Susanna is held in esteem in the narrative for her willingness to be faithful and to place her trust in God.

Susanna, a married woman, is described as one who is very beautiful and refined (vv. 2, 31), which prepares the reader for the judges' lust for her. No mere beauty, her character is further developed. She is learned in the Torah of Moses, having been taught by her parents, and she fears God. When confronted by the judges' plot to either be raped by them or face their unjust accusations that she had sexual relations with another unidentifiable man, she responds with dignity. Powerless in the face of men of authority and prestige, whom the community respect, she risks their unjust charges, which leads to her death, rather than "sin in the sight of the Lord" (v. 23). Although the judges imply that she will escape death only by consenting to have sex with them and thus avoiding their accusations, she refers to the Torah by claiming that participation in their crime would be her true death.

When confronted with the accusation of adultery, Susanna turns to God. Just as the judges begin to testify, she looks toward heaven with trust, even though her eyes are filled with tears. When she is sentenced to death, she again turns to God in prayer. This time, God responds by filling the young boy Daniel with the heavenly spirit. Daniel shrewdly unmasks the judges' wickedness and chastises the assembly for not interrogating the "witnesses." In contrast to Susanna, who knows Torah and who trusts in God, the judges, who are expected to have these qualities, act as though there were no Torah. They are described as wicked, lustful, and plotting, having "abandoned God and justice" (v. 9). Even when Susanna has refused them, they take the opportunity to unveil her at her trial so that they might again exercise their voyeurism. When Daniel questions them, he reveals that the first judge had been rendering unjust judgments all along and that the second judge had been intimidating and violating women previously!

As justice is served at the end of this engaging plot, the narrator states that the entire assembly "raised a great shout and blessed God, who saves those who hope in him" (v. 60). Susanna's behavior becomes the paradigm for steadfastness to Torah and faith and hope in God. Still, Susanna is not recognized as fully at the conclusion of the story as most current readers might like. The

183

account culminates with the remark that Daniel—not Susanna—has the great reputation. In the context of the story, Daniel was God's mouthpiece, so perhaps this is not a surprising conclusion. Nonetheless, the reader will remember that because of Susanna's trust in God and her ensuing deliverance, the entire community saw the consequences of faith. In addition, because of her prayer and faith, the wickedness of the judges, their abandonment of Torah, their unjust judgments, and their violence against other women were ended.

Retelling the Story

She came into my office on a dreary Monday in April. She'd called my secretary a few days before—said she had to see me right away. I don't get too many new clients out of the blue like that; these days I mostly handle real estate closings and bank foreclosures—that sort of thing. I haven't seen the inside of a courtroom in months. I've purposely stayed away from litigation. To tell the truth, I saw a few too many cases go the wrong way, and I figured I was losing my touch. My name's Danielle.

Her name was Susanna, and she was beautiful. I don't usually notice that about other women, but I was in my favorite suit and I'd actually had my hair done that week, and she made me feel like I was a kid in a T-shirt. She carried herself with an ease that some exceptionally beautiful women have: yes, they know everyone's looking at them, but it doesn't bother them. The only uneasy part of her was her eyes; I could tell she was frightened.

"I heard you're very good on rape cases," she told me in a rush. "I need all the help I can get."

I invited her to sit down and tell me her story.

"This is confidential, right? If it got into the papers or on TV. . . "

"I promise you whatever you tell me goes no further than this office," I reassured her. "But if you decide to prosecute, the media might be involved. Let's take it one step at a time. Why don't we just talk about it first." I leaned back and waited for her to get comfortable.

> Some say that the young Daniel was a eunuch in the royal court when he came forward to prove the virtuous Susanna innocent. Perhaps this was supposed to give him a special objectivity in uncovering the truth about sexual matters. (*Mimekor Yisrael*, pp. 205-6)

She sat and began twisting the strap on her purse. "I'm married to a judge." She told me his name—a well-known man with a good reputation among lawyers.

"Saturday night some friends invited me to a party. A lot of my husband's associates were there, some friends of friends . . . and Congressman R——'s son Michael, the lawyer who's made a name for himself this year."

I nodded. I knew who she meant. Every town has its prominent citizens, and the Senator's family was particularly well-known. His son had been elected to city government right out of law school. He was as ambitious as they come.

"Well, it got late, and a group of us decided to go for a walk down by the shore. My friends Janet and Jay were with me, and Michael and his cousin Robert or something. . . . I'm not sure of his name. Anyway, Jay has a bad knee, and so they turned back and I kept walking with . . . them."

She stopped and took a few deep breaths. I offered her a glass of water, and she continued.

"Well, at first the two of them were complimenting me . . . on my dress, my perfume. I started getting uncomfortable and suggested we walk back to the party. That was when Michael told me he'd admired me ever since he first met me, and wouldn't I just like to have a quickie with him and his cousin and wasn't that a great idea? And I said 'Thank you, no, that wasn't a great idea,' and I started walking back, but the cousin got in front of me and grabbed my arm and said they'd tell my husband that I slept with both of them if I didn't— so wasn't it just better if I did and just enjoyed myself.

"I tried to pull away and run, but they held me down and ripped my dress . . . I guess I was screaming because they ran away . . . and then I was alone."

She stopped and wiped her eyes, then looked at her hands as she continued.

"When I got home I threw my dress in the garbage and showered for about an hour. Then I made sure all the doors were locked and took the phone off the hook and cried until I fell asleep. My husband wasn't due home for a few more days. I called a friend and said I might be in trouble and did she know who I could call. She gave me your name."

I'd heard the same story before, but it never fails to get to me. An unreported rape, and she'd destroyed the evidence. The only thing different about Susanna's story was the possibility of blackmail—and the fact that some very well-known names were involved. She was right to be afraid of the media; if this was made public, they'd have a field day. But if she wanted to prosecute, there was no other way to do it.

"Is your husband home yet?"

"Tonight," she said wryly. "He called from the airport this morning to tell me everything was okay."

"What are you planning to tell him?"

"The truth. We've always told each other the truth." She stated it sadly but simply, as if everyone always told "the truth."

"And you'd like to press charges?"

"I think so, but I'm not sure. Their family . . . their reputation . . . my husband's reputation . . . I just don't know."

We talked some more, and I urged her to discuss the whole incident with her husband. Was it worth having her name out there for news writers to pounce on? Or was it worse letting the men go unpunished? I wanted Susanna and her husband to decide together—they'd have to face the questioning and conjecturing as a team. It's hard to know what a defense lawyer might dig up. Or a judge or jury decide.

Back in biblical times a woman who was accused of being unfaithful to her husband might be stoned to death. Now it's easier. She just might get her name and photo plastered on the front page of every paper; have every columnist in town making her out to be a tramp or a fool or worse; have her family and friends turn against her.

A beautiful woman like Susanna, who simply talks about "the truth"; a plain woman just trying to get by; a young kid who gets in over her head; I've heard the story before, too many times.

I told her if she wanted to prosecute, I'd take the case.

(Betty Lehrman)

A Samaritan version of this story identifies Susanna as the daughter of Amram the High Priest at Mt. Gerizim. The two men who falsely accuse her were visitors on a religious pilgrimage. In this version, Susanna escapes by telling the men that she wants to go and put on prettier clothes for them. She leaves and never returns. Instead, she prays to God for help. (*Mimekor Yisrael,* pp. 206-7)

Judith

Judith risks her virtue and her life in order to save her people from foreign domination.

The Story

When Judith heard how the people, demoralized by the shortage of water, had made shameful demands on Ozias the magistrate, and how he had given them his oath to surrender the town to the Assyrians at the end of five days, she sent her maid who had charge of everything she owned to ask Ozias, Chabris, and Charmis, the elders of the town, to come and see her.

On their arrival she said: 'Listen to me, magistrates of Bethulia. It was wrong of you to speak as you did to the people today, binding yourselves and God in a solemn contract to surrender the town to our enemies unless the Lord sends relief within so many days. Who are you to put God to the test at a time like this, and to usurp his role in human affairs? It is the Lord Almighty you are now putting to the proof! Will you never understand? You are unable to plumb the depths of the human heart or grasp the way the mind works; how then can you fathom the Maker of mortal beings? How can you know God's mind and understand his thought? No, my friends, do not provoke the anger of the Lord our God. For even if he does not choose to help us within the five days, he has the power to shield us at any time he pleases, or equally he can let us be destroyed by our enemies. It is not for you to impose conditions on the Lord our God, because God will neither yield to threats nor be bargained with like a mere mortal. So while we wait for the deliverance which is his to give, let us appeal to him for help. If he sees fit, he will hear us.

'At the present day there is not one of our tribes or clans, districts or towns, that worships man-made gods, or has done so within living memory. This did take place in days gone by, and that was why our forefathers were abandoned to slaughter and pillage, and great was their downfall at the hand of the enemy. We, however, acknowledge no god but the Lord, and so have confidence that he will not spurn us or any of our nation. If we should lose Bethulia, then all Judaea will be lost; the temple will be sacked, and God will hold us responsible for its desecration. The slaughter and deportation of our fellow-countrymen and the devastation of our ancestral land will bring his judgment on our heads, wherever among the Gentiles we become slaves. Our masters will regard us with disgust and contempt. There will be no happy ending to our servitude, no return to favour the Lord.

'My friends, let us now set an example to our fellow-countrymen, for their lives depend on us, and with us rests the fate of the temple, its precincts, and the altar. Despite our peril let us give thanks to the Lord our God, for he is putting us to the test as he did our forefathers. Remember how he dealt with Abraham, and how he tested Isaac, and what happened to Jacob in Syrian Mesopotamia while he was working as a shepherd for his uncle Laban. The Lord is subjecting us to the same fiery ordeal by which he tested their loyalty, not taking vengeance on us: it is as a warning that he scourges his worshippers.'

Ozias replied, 'You have spoken from the wisdom of your heart, and what you say no one can deny. This is not the first time you have given proof of your wisdom; throughout your life we have all recognized your good sense and sound judgment. But the people were desperate with thirst, and drove us to make this promise and bind ourselves by an oath we may not break. You are a devout woman; pray for us now and ask the Lord to send the rain to fill our cisterns, and then we shall be faint no more.'

'Listen to me,' said Judith. 'I am going to do something which will be remembered among our countrymen for all generations. Be at the gate tonight; I shall go out with my maid and, before the day on which you have promised to surrender the town to our enemies, the Lord will deliver Israel by my hand. But do not question me about my plan; I shall tell you nothing until I have accomplished what I mean to do.' Ozias and the magistrates said to her, 'Go with our blessing, and may you have the guidance of the Lord God as you take vengeance on our enemies.'

They then left her roof-shelter and returned to their posts. . . .

When it grew late, Holophernes' servants made haste to withdraw, and Bagoas closed the tent from outside, shutting out the attendants from his master's presence, and they went off to their beds; the banquet had lasted so long that they were all exhausted. Judith was now alone in the tent, with Holophernes lying sprawled on his bed, dead drunk. Judith had told her maid to stand outside the sleeping apartment and wait for her to go out as she did on other days; she had said that she would be going out to pray, and had explained this to Bagoas also.

When all had left and not a soul remained, Judith stood beside Holophernes' bed and prayed silently: 'O Lord, God of all power, look favourably now on what I am doing to bring glory to Jerusalem, for this is the moment to come to the aid of your heritage and to prosper my plan for crushing the enemies who have attacked us.' She went to the bed-rail beside Holophernes' head, reached down his sword, and drawing close to the bed she gripped him by the hair. 'Now give me strength, O Lord, God of Israel,' she said, and struck at his neck twice with all her might and cut off his head. . . .

The people were all astounded at what she had done; and bowing in worship to God, they spoke with one voice: 'Praise be to you, our God, who has this day humiliated the enemies of your people!' Ozias addressed Judith: 'Daughter, the blessing of God Most High rests on you more than on any other woman on earth; praise be to the Lord God who created heaven and earth; under his guidance you struck off the head of the leader of our enemies. As long as men

188

commemorate the power of God, the
sure hope which inspired you will never
fade from their minds. May God make
your deed redound to your honour for
ever, and may he shower blessings on
you! You risked your life for our nation
when it was faced with humiliation. Boldly you went to meet the disaster that
threatened us, and firmly you held to
God's straight road.' All the people
responded, 'Amen, Amen.'

Comments on the Story

The story of Judith, written during the second–first centuries B.C.E., provides an exceptional portrayal of a pious and courageous Jew who saves her
people from the impending destruction of Holophernes, the general of Nebuchadnezzar's army. The work is riddled with historical inaccuracies; Nebuchadnezzar is described as king of the Assyrians, whereas he was king of
Babylon, and as ruler during the period after the Exile, whereas he actually was
in power when Jerusalem fell to his armies. Some scholars suggest that these
obvious inaccuracies are used to define the work as fiction or as a more timeless narrative. Whether the historical errors were deliberate, the account serves
to offer an engaging account of a woman devoted to God and to her people and
presents a theology that stresses fidelity to God and God's covenantal stipula-
tions, even when it is uncertain that God will come to the rescue of a subdued
or vanquished Israel.

The first seven chapters of the book of Judith portray an invincible
Assyrian army under the leadership of the ruthless Holophernes. They are
poised to attack Bethulia, a city that holds the gateway to Jerusalem (the
identity of Bethulia is currently unknown). The army has cut off the water
supply to the city, and its people are so weakened that they demand their
leaders to surrender. The leaders respond that if God does not deliver them
within five days, they will agree. But Judith enters to provide an alternative
plan.

Judith is described throughout the book as a woman of exceptional beauty,
virtue, and piety. She wears sackcloth, fasts, and honors the sabbath and Jewish festivals. Although she is a widow, she has a life of some independence:
She is wealthy, manages her own property, and has servants. Upon hearing of
the town leaders' plan, she is outraged and summons them. As an indication of
her prestige and as a future indicator of her ability to accomplish her strategy,
the rulers appear at her home. She is forthright in her speech to them, chastis-
ing them for testing God. Echoing the same sentiment found in the book of
Job, she points out that if the leaders cannot understand the depths of the
human mind, how can they presume to know God's purposes? Her theology
keeps the freedom of God intact. She does not presume to control God and
knows that no amount of fasting, prayer, or pleading will threaten God to act.

189

For Judith, who practices these acts of piety, they obviously have intrinsic value. She does not say they should be dismissed; rather, she emphasizes that they cannot be used to force God's hand. She concludes that "he will hear our voice, if it pleases him" (8:17). Some of her statements echo Deuteronomic theology, which holds that Israel experiences defeat when it is unfaithful to God.

Nevertheless, she believes that the present threat from the Assyrians is not due to any idolatry on the part of the present generation, but rather, "the Lord scourges those who are close to him in order to admonish them" (8:27). Thus, although she hopes and prays for deliverance, she understands that God's providence is beyond human scrutiny.

When the elder Uzziah responds to her, he acknowledges her wisdom and righteousness, yet insists that his original plan be followed—that the people wait five days. Moreover, he adds another stipulation. Whereas previously he had stated that the people should wait five days for an unqualified deliverance from God, now he specifies that God should send rain! Judith responds immediately by stating that she has her own plan. She withholds the details, simply indicating that the elders allow her to exit the town. It is appropriate that the plan's specifics not be announced, first of all because it is obvious that Uzziah and the elders lack understanding, and second because it builds suspense for the reader. Whatever Judith is undertaking, it must be dangerous. She is an unarmed woman, a widow, and an enemy of the Assyrians!

Judith first prepares herself by praying, acknowledging the saving God of the oppressed and God of her ancestors. The reader gains a clue to her plan when she prays that her "deceitful words bring wound and bruise" (9:13) on those intent on Israel's destruction. She makes herself look beautiful and prepares her own food and drink, giving the provisions to the maid who accompanies her. The significance of these details soon becomes apparent. She uses her beauty to gain acceptance into Holophernes' quarters; her food enables her to remain faithful to the laws of *kashrut* when he insists on her presence at the banquet, and the maid's presence and the food sack enable her planned assassination of Holophernes to go undetected.

When Judith meets Holophernes, she speaks words of deceit, which also are replete with double entendre. "If you follow out the words of your servant," she confides. "God will accomplish something through you, and my lord will not fail to achieve his purposes" (11:6). Her fidelity to the covenant enables her to set a trap. She promises that she will get important strategic information for Holophernes by praying every night and that God will reveal when her people will be unable to withstand an onslaught. She says she cannot eat his food because of *kashrut* and has brought her own provisions. Her beauty prompts the king to desire her immensely, and when he invites her to his banquet he is not surprised that she brings her own food and wine. Because she drinks before

190

him, he consumes more alcohol than he ever had in his life and lies unconscious in his bed (12:19).

Now Judith can take action. She uses her maid to stand guard. Praying for God's help, Judith cuts off Holophernes' head with only two blows and puts it in the food sack her maid has been holding. They are able to escape because when they exit the tent it can be assumed they are going for their customary evening prayers. When Judith returns to her people, all praise God for their deliverance.

Out of context, Holophernes' decapitation seems macabre, but in the story it is a strategic move by Judith to confound the Assyrian army. When the army discovers the horror they flee in a panic. Judith commands the Israelite army to attack them at daybreak, and the soldiers are victorious over a retreating, disorganized army. In language reminiscent of the Song of Miriam, the women dance and all the people sing a song of praise with Judith, extolling the God of Israel, who fights for the oppressed.

Judith's victory is reminiscent of those of other famous women in the Hebrew Bible. Like Miriam, she leads her people in a song of praise to God. Paralleling Deborah, she plans strategy for the troops. Like Jael, she assassinates the general of the army of Israel's enemies. Like Esther, she attends a banquet of an official in all her finery to plan a strategy to save her people. Yet Judith stands out because she acts so completely without the help of men. There is no Moses, Barak, or Mordecai to assist her. Her praise is singular as well. The book concludes with a reference to the fame she had for the rest of her long life and the continuing results of her victory. Even her virtue is extolled; she remains a widow and sets her maid free. For many American women today, the depiction of Judith as a political assassin who uses feminine wiles to entrap the enemy may seem distasteful, but her independence, willingness to risk her life for a higher cause, and devotion to her traditions and her God still can inspire.

Retelling the Story

Tel Aviv 1991.

My name is Judith, and I don't know what to do.

Last year I rocked my new baby in my arms, and the world disappeared. I was caught in a cocoon of love and warmth. The minutes and hours passed as we rocked, smiled, and sang. When my baby finally fell asleep and I placed her in the crib, my heart seemed too full of love. My days were filled with diaper changes and beautiful little socks that were always missing their mates and visits from my family. But now the world has turned upside down.

My name is Judith, and I don't know what to do.

The siren screams, and we gather the baby and run to the basement, where the doors are sealed and there are no windows to let in poison gas. We make a game of putting on the gas masks, but she cries and we try not to cry and we are so, so tired. We shiver until the all-clear sounds and we can go back up to bed. In the morning, there is broken glass; yesterday part of our neighbor's house was gone. There is no school, no work; maybe soon there will be no water.

One story has Judith going to Jerusalem to visit a ruler named Selucius. When he heard how beautiful this young Jewish woman was, he consented to see her. After she told him that she had come to win his friendship, he invited her to a feast. After having much to eat and drink, Selucius made lewd advances to Judith. She pretends to respond favorably, but tells him that she is just completing her period and must go through a ritual bath (*mikva*) before having sexual relations. She asked if he would tell his guards not to hinder her and her handmaid as they left the palace. He agreed and sent word that she should not be stopped as she left his presence. After everyone else had been sent away, Selucius became so drunk that he passed out. Judith cut off his head and carried it out of the city in a bag. No one stopped her—by order of the very ruler whose head she carried with her. (*Mimekor Yisrael*, pp. 258-59)

In the days of Judith, my namesake, there were wars. In my parents' time there were wars. Why was I so foolish to think that I was safe, so warm in the love of my husband and my child?

Judith saw her city besieged, surrounded. The enemy cut off the water, and the people began to die of thirst. The rulers were impotent, trying vainly to bargain with God. Judith didn't meekly accept her fate—she devised a plan. She walked into the enemy's camp, enchanting everyone with her beauty. Then she drank Holophernes under the table and cut off his head, saving Israel.

Now my city is besieged. The officials are impotent. The rest of the world tries to help, but the missiles shriek overhead. We are pawns in a war that is not even ours. The faces of our enemy stare at us from the television screens in our living rooms. We can't walk to this enemy's camp; it is a plane-flight away. The weapons and armies are huge, fueled by international cartels and "covert political operations." And I don't have a plan and I'm not beautiful and I can't drink. What can I do? What would Judith do? Will Israel be saved?

When my parents first came here Israel was still called Palestine. My father's family fled from Germany as Hitler came to power. They joined a group of Russian, Hungarian, Persian, and Iraqi Jews in founding a kibbutz. My mother's family came from Russia. They left after the pogroms in 1896.

192

My mother was a Sabra, born here. My parents met while harvesting grapes, and the families were all concerned by a German Jew marrying a Russian Jew. Such a terrible match, my grandmother thought, two such different cultures! My two brothers were born during Israel's War of Independence. My family emigrated to the United States, and I was born there and brought up in a suburb outside of New York City. My childhood was full of baseball games, hot dogs, orange soda, and fireworks on the Fourth of July.

I was in high school when the 1967 war began. We watched the news on TV, and as different places came on the screen my parents told us how they'd once had an apartment near that gate . . . they'd shopped over there where the bullets were flying . . . they had friends near that part of Jerusalem. . . .

After college I came to Israel. I wanted to see what it was like. I ate olives in the Arab market in Jerusalem. I sipped *café au lait* on Dizingoff Street in Tel Aviv. I went camping with friends in the Sinai. I loved the warmth and variety of the people, and the sense of purpose in carving out a home in such an ancient land.

I got an apartment and a job. I met my husband at a film festival. He was brought up on baseball and orange soda, too, near Chicago. We talked about art. We got married and had a child. Sure, we had friends who'd been in the army; my friend David had even fought in Beirut. But somehow we thought the wars were over.

Now there is another madman in power, another Nebuchadnezzar who wants the world to bow to him. Forces are marshalled against him, but still we hide in cellars, afraid of the death raining down on us. I want my child to grow up healthy and unafraid, sip *café au lait*, talk about art. I don't want her childhood to slip away in fear. Each day is an eternity. When will it end?

My name is Judith, and I don't know what to do. *(Betty Lehrman)*

Another story has the king ordering Judith to marry him, and at first she seems to respond positively. But after she has cut off his head and is making her escape, she runs into an obstacle. The guard at the gate will not let her pass. She tells him that she carries the king's head with her, but he does not believe her. It just so happens that a courtier who has been sentenced to hang by his hands at the gate for criticizing the king is nearby. Judith pulls out the bloody head, and the courtier confirms that it belonged to the king. When word spread that this young Jewish woman had singlehandedly defeated the king, all his followers fled in terror. (*Mimekor Yisrael*, pp. 259-60)

Index of Readings from
The Revised Common Lectionary

Index of Midrashim

Genesis Rabbah

Exodus Rabbah

Leviticus Rabbah